ADVENTURES IN WASHINGTON

BY ARCHIE SATTERFIELD

The Writing Works, Inc.
Mercer Island, Washington

Gordon Soules Book Publishers
Vancouver, B.C., Canada

To Chet and Pearl Bell

Chet overworked me in the field, but Pearl nursed me back to health at meal time.

Cover: Hiking On Hurricane Ridge

Library of Congress Cataloging in Publication Data

Satterfield, Archie.
    Adventures in Washington.

    Includes index.
        1. Washington (State)—Description and travel—
1951-   —Guide-books. 2. Satterfield, Archie.
3. Washington (State)—History, Local. I. Title.
F889.3.S27 1978   917.97'04'4   78-26538
ISBN 0-916076-23-7

photo credits

Jan Fardell: 20, 25, 27, 31, 32, 36, 65, 66, 67, 89,
    96 (left)
Washington State Travel: 7, 23, 33, 59 (left, 78, 79,
    82, 107, 110, 113, 132, 133
U.S. Forest Service: 43, 46, 56, 69
Family Adventures: 63
Bureau of Reclamation: 68, 110
Washington State Ferries: 72-73
Washington Department of Game: 90, 91, 94
Seattle Parks and Recreation: 96 (left)
Asahel Curtis: 111
Soil Conservation Service: 116
Seattle Opera Association: 125
Seattle Center: 127

All other photos, including the front and back
covers, are by the author.

Copyright © 1978 by Archie Satterfield
All Rights Reserved
Manufactured in the United States
Published by The Writing Works, Inc.
            7438 S.E. 40th Street
                Mercer Island, Washington 98040
ISBN: 0-916076-23-7 (U.S.)
Library of Congress Catalog Card Number:
Published in Canada by Gordon Soules Book Publishers
    1118-355 Burrard Street
    Vancouver, B.C., Canada V6C 2G8
ISBN: 0-919574-32-7 (Canada)

Contents

I FIRST came to Washington in the summer of 1957 when one of my brothers arranged for me to work on a wheat farm during summer vacation from college in Missouri. My only previous experience with Washington was a very brief visit to Bremerton while I was in the Navy. Few of us went ashore, and my impressions of the state revolved around lots of salt water, tall evergreens growing down to the hightide mark, a nasty sea off the coast that gave me my only brush with *mal de mer*. And mountains. Lots of mountains.

So when my brother called and said he had a job for me on a wheat farm, I was skeptical. I knew from my Kansas and Nebraska experiences that wheat does not grow well in damp, foggy weather. I was certain he was talking about the small stump ranches with wheat competing with fern and salal for growing space. In my ignorance, I thought the stumps, brush, and rain must be very rough on machinery.

But I was landlocked in Rockford, Illinois, that summer waiting for the vegetable harvest to begin and spending the remainder of my last G.I. check. So I agreed and caught a bus back to St. Louis to pack more clothes and bid goodbye again to a girl who didn't seem terribly unhappy about my leaving.

I arrived in Ritzville late at night, disoriented from going without sleep the first two nights on the bus across the Great Plains and deserts, then sleeping most of the way through Oregon and up through eastern Washington. I was delivered to the farm where I would spend the following three summers, and went to bed that night ignorant of the geography outside.

I was absolutely astonished when I went outside the next morning. The only trees in sight were those planted around the house as a windbreak. The nearest water was probably 200 feet underground and none on the surface for 40 miles. The hills, rolling and sculpted into humps over the centuries, undulated off beyond the horizon, and before breakfast was over, the wind was blowing its steady stream out of the southwest, hot and persistent. The day was already desert-warm, and the sky was taking on that flat, ash color of a scorcher in the making.

I became intimately acquainted with the wheat country during the next three summers and never made a trip to what everyone there calls "the coast." With my employers, Chet and Pearl Bell, I toured the wheat country. I met everyone in Adams County and part of Whitman County, it seemed. They took me to pancake breakfasts in Benge and to family picnics at Ritzville.

And we worked. I plowed, fertilized, and seeded spring wheat where winter wheat had either frozen out or been blown out the previous fall. I rod-weeded and helped overhaul combines and drills. I drove trucks and combines during harvest, and one summer, the first, I went up near Spokane to work for another farmer who was an alcoholic and had me driving a truck with no door on the driver's side, one brake that worked (on the right front if I remember correctly), and then cheated me out of $2 a day when the summer ended.

After that, I stayed around Ritzville and Washtucna where I knew people and worked for the Bells when they needed me and other farmers when the Bells didn't. During all this time the farmers tried to talk me into staying in Washington and completing school at what was then called Washington State College in Pullman. But I stayed in Missouri, in part because the girl who didn't seem to mind my leaving also didn't seem to mind when I returned.

I still cannot explain the events of that night in Columbia, Missouri, when I decided to leave. I had just enrolled for the second semester and was apparently quite happy at the University of Missouri. But about midnight one night I suddenly decided to leave, a not unusual phenomenon among students I'm told. The next morning I packed up, went to the university's admissions offices for a refund on my tuition and with that headed out of town. From St. Louis I called Chet Bell and asked if there was any kind of work around Washtucna for me that time of year. He said to come on out and we'd find something.

My little 1950 Chevrolet coupe was loaded with books and records so heavily that the rear springs were almost flat on the axle, and the front reared so high that I had to drive with the lights on low beam all the time. I had less than $100 and couldn't afford motels and restaurant meals, so I stopped in grocery stores and drove day and night. At night I would drive until I got sleepy, then pull over and sleep until the car cooled down to the temperatures outside, which was below freezing. The cold would awaken me and I would continue. I arrived at the Bell's home with $8 in my pocket and a terrible taste in my mouth. They put me to bed for the rest of that day, and the next day I went to work on another farm and spent the spring wondering what I had done with my life.

That was my last summer on wheat farms. I was accepted at the University of Washington in the fall of 1959 and drove over Snoqualmie Pass for the first time, a bit apprehensive about my choice of a new school and a new city.

Any doubts I had about my choices were dispelled simply by my arrival. I drove down from Snoqualmie that Sunday afternoon, dropping steadily toward sea level through the thickest evergreen forest I had ever been in, and arrived on the floating bridge between Mercer Island and Seattle during a spectacular sunset. I knew I was entering a city that was the most beautiful I had ever seen, which at that time included all those west of the Mississippi plus Honolulu and Acapulco. Seattle seemed fresh and subtle, new. Before I had found an apartment, I wrote friends in Missouri that I was here to stay.

The entire state gave credence to my Midwestern belief that the future for us all was in the West. It had never occurred to me, or most of my friends, to leave Missouri for the East. To us, the West seemed new and clean, the East old, worn out and dirty.

I have never regretted that decision, even during the dark, damp winters when the desert looks so appealing; during the autumns without the incredible colors of the Midwest and Northeast; or during the summers when we often wear sweaters for our backyard sojourns. Ever since that September evening I have been committed to traveling Washington and learning its many regions, its nooks and crannies. Like many residents, I have learned to break the state into manageable regions, or "countries": The Okanogan Country, the Wheat Country, the Palouse Country, Coulee Country, Big Bend Country, and one slowly gaining usage, the Lewis and Clark Country.

Those divisions are more popular east of the Cascade Range, while on the western side we speak of valleys or peninsulas: Skagit Valley, Grays Harbor area, Long Beach Peninsula, Olympic Peninsula, Kitsap Peninsula, San Juans, Cowlitz Valley, and so forth.

In addition, there are smaller regions such as the Horse Heaven Hills, the Yakima Valley, the Tri-Cities area, and Pend Oreille.

It has been suggested—and even proposed by some malcontents—that Washington should never have been made into a single state, that it should have been divided right down the middle of the Cascade Range. Geographically, and to an extent politically, the idea has merit because the two sides of the state are so radically different. The population has a heavy tilt to the west. The east is primarily agricultural; the west is oriented to timber, manufacturing and shipping. The west gets too much rain for many residents' taste, and the east doesn't get enough. The west gets most of the state and federal funds and the east feels left out, ignored.

But for the in-state traveler, these differences are benefits. One can drive an hour from the major metropolitan areas along Puget Sound and be in a wilderness setting, two hours and be in a desert. A surprising number of Washington residents never travel beyond the state boundaries because they feel there is nothing elsewhere that the state doesn't already have. Like New York cab drivers, the horizon holds no mysteries for them.

I have been more fortunate than many newcomers (after all these years I still feel rather new) because my work on newspapers has permitted me to travel extensively throughout the state and the nature of my work necessitates meeting and talking with people everywhere I go. Consequently, there are few parts of the state I haven't traveled—either working or with my family.

This book is a result of all that traveling for the newspapers and for our own pleasure. Originally this was going to be a straightforward guide to the state, but several of those have been written already and there is little to add to them. Instead, I decided to go back through my files and see if the stories I have written over the years held up well enough with the passage of time to combine them into an anthology. Unfortunately, with the emphasis of newspaper writing on the exact present, most of them did not. However, by reshaping them, and in many cases updating them, I found that the basic story content was there. I have simply recast them into a less timely form.

February, 1979, is my 20th anniversary in Washington, with one year out of residence while living just across the line in Oregon. Some readers may be disappointed in the title, *Adventures in Washington*, since some of the so-called adventures are rather sedentary. I may be stretching the definition of "adventure," a bit, but I will remember the afternoon I listened to Bach and watched the play of rain and sun on Puget Sound as one of my most satisfying adventures in Washington.

So—this isn't a travel guide in the purest sense of the word. It is, however, a travel book because it is about different places and different people. For the reader's convenience, an appendix lists the major events of the state and orients the reader to at least know the story is set in the rain belt and not in a desert.

I have avoided recommending—or warning against—places to stay and eat. Any private enterprise, such as a guide service, a resort, cafe, tour, or hotel is mentioned here for information only. A mention does not represent a recommendation. Some places have not lived up to my personal expectations, but those same places have made other people almost delirious with pleasure. I have tried to suggest things to do and places to see that involve no more expenditure than driving there and back. Most of us are so destination-oriented that we have lost our ability to simply go for a drive or a weekend trip for no better reason than it seemed like a good idea at the time. We take too little time to amble through the countryside, and I include myself in this condemnation. Yet some of the most memorable people I've met were those we just happened upon and decided to stop and chat with for awhile.

Some stories, then, aren't exciting. Some may not even be particularly informative. Yet I remember those people better than I remember best-selling authors I've interviewed, or even nasty characters who helped turn weekends into disasters. If I were fancy, I would borrow James Joyce's term for some such stories and call them epiphanies, or the slightly less fancy, vignettes. Whatever they may be finally called, I hope nobody calls them dull.

Approaches to the State

About midway through my career at *The Seattle Times*, I wrote a story for the magazine about the three college professors who had the greatest impact on me. One was an Elizabethan scholar at the University of Missouri named Hardin Craig, and the other two were University of Washington teachers—Thomas Presley, the great Civil War scholar at the University of Washington, and Herman Deutsch, a Washington State University professor who taught a summer course in Pacific Northwest history at the University of Washington.

Perhaps more than anyone else, Deutsch put the Northwest on my mental and spiritual map in that abbreviated summer quarter, even though my grade was not inspiring. If anything, it proved that grades do not always represent the true value of a course.

Deutsch put people into history. He told us of the absurdities of Northwest history, such as the political events surrounding martial law during the Indian War of the 1850s in Pierce County. And he told us of the heroic figures, including one man who drove a small herd of cattle over the old Snoqualmie wagon road, sold them, and used the money to finance his college education in Seattle.

After his course, we came away filled with the power and the gloom of the Olympic coast, where the Russians, Spanish, and English traveled and traded for decades before the Oregon Country became a territory and then two states. This, combined with my experience aboard a ship off the Washington coast several years before, provided continuity for my Olympics' experience and an appreciation for those who fought to keep the coast wild. Even though thousands of people hike across the wooden planks to the archaeological dig at Cape Alava, and hundreds hike along the coastal strip of Olympic National Park each year, still the coast retains its wildness and danger. And if I never again hike that coast, it is comforting to know there is at least one place left in the state much the same as it was when the first Russians sailed along it, needing a place to land and establish a farm for the posts in Alaska, but terrified of the forbidding shoreline.

THE OLYMPICS AND THE COAST

LIKE the early explorers of the Olympic Mountains, we have only skirted them and have never gone on the long hikes deep into the real wilderness and up to the glaciers. We know what we've been missing because the places we've visited around the edge of Olympic National Park have been among the most interesting and beautiful in the state.

The Olympics comprise one of America's last and most beautiful wildernesses, and it has attracted some of the most dedicated protectors of any place in the West. Not only have they fought off attempts to decrease the size of the park so its virgin timber can be cut, they have been succesful in having it enlarged from time to time.

Although only two hours from the heavy population areas, the Olympics retain a sense of remoteness. They are a bit more difficult to reach than the Cascades, and few people decide on the spur of the moment to visit them.

Even the well-publicized romances have a rugged air to them, such as that of John "Iron Man" Huelsdonk, a Midwesterner who discovered the Olympics on his own terms, filed for a homestead far up the Hoh River Valley, then went back home for a bride. They lived happily ever after far from civilization. Huelsdonk earned the nickname for his phenomenal strength, and perhaps the most popular story about him was the time he was seen carrying a cast-iron cook stove up the trail toward home. Someone asked him if it wasn't hard to carry, and he only complained that the sack (or sacks, depending on who tells the story) of flour inside the stove kept shifting around.

There's something about the Olympics that brings out the heroic in many people. A filmmaker, Herb Crisler, kept a vow he made 50 years earlier when he was a young man of 30. He said he was going to return and hike all the way across the Olympics again when he was 80. And he did.

Forks, one of the largest towns in the Olympics and a bastion of loggers, is a pleasant and clean place inland a few miles from the ocean. It is probably the safest town in the state for people who mind their own business. For those intent on mischief, the loggers have their own solution, and outside troublemakers are made to feel distinctly unwelcome. This was brought to the nation's attention one Fourth of July when some outsiders decided they would have a little fun at the local people's expense. They made the mistake of trying to rough up the local police, and as one resident later explained, "We don't like to have our cops bent," and the donnybrook was on. The loggers live by the Gary Cooper code: "If you talk loud, be prepared to back it up. Mind your manners and your own business and nothing will happen to you."

Relics of the past dot the mountaintops and beaches. Scattered along the wild coast—one of the wildest in America—are bits and pieces of shipwrecks dating back to the arrival of the white traders. Some of the worst shipwrecks in West Coast history occurred along the Olympic coast. Some vessels got caught in storms too close to the shore or simply lost their way and turned into the Strait of Juan de Fuca before they were really there. Hikers along the beach can find plaques for some of the worst disasters, such as the Norwegian Memorial on the beach near the tip of Lake Ozette. A bark went aground there about the turn of the century when the pilot mistakenly headed for a light that was a beach cabin and not a lighthouse or bouy marker for the strait several miles north.

In the early 1970s, another chapter was added to the Norwegian story. Viggo Marcussen, then 79, came to the memorial from his native Norway to pay his only visit to his father's grave. He came as a guest of the timber company, ITT-Rayonier. He was helicoptered out to the headstone and placed a wreath on the grave. His father, knowing the ship was sinking beneath him in the heavy seas, gave his life jacket to a young seaman who lived. Marcussen's father remained aboard while his bark was slowly ground into driftwood that stormy night.

Other markers, none named, date only as far back as World War II when fears of a Japanese invasion prompted the military to line the coast with gun emplacements and send foot and horse patrols up and down the beach to watch for submarines and aircraft. Many of the concrete bunkers remain, almost hidden by the dense underbrush that grows almost as fast as tropical plants in rainfall that sometimes reaches 250 inches a year.

4

We found a cabin built for aircraft spotters on a hike from **Lake Crescent**. The cabin, in remarkably good condition in spite of windows being broken, stands on the promontory atop Pyramid Peak above Lake Crescent. Much of the telephone line is still strung from trees along the trail. There were dozens of such lookouts during the war, scattered all over the Olympics. One is reminded of members of a cargo culture, waiting for something that never appeared.

Lake Crescent is on the edge of the Olympics, and we have never found a more beautiful lake anywhere in the state, in spite of a twisting road that follows the entire length of the southern shore with log trucks barreling along it amid the parade of campers and trailers during summer months.

No matter what time of day or season, Lake Crescent never quite looks the same from one hour to the next. It is undoubtedly the most photogenic lake in the area, and I have exposed many rolls of

film there with only limited success because mere photographs cannot capture the mood of a place when that mood depends on silence, temperature, or the sounds of birds calling and water lapping against a rock.

Probably the most impressive viewpoint in the Olympics is from the visitor center and trail along the crest of **Hurricane Ridge**. The barren ridge, reached by driving south out of Port Angeles, is alive with wildflowers during the summer months. Early in the summer, snow banks still touch the trail and dot the high meadows where trees do not grow. From the ridge you experience one of the most spectacular views of the range. Another

Crab pots and abandoned piling are part of the landscape of the mudflats at Nahcotta, on the Willapa Bay side of Long Beach Peninsula.

A footbridge helps keep the feet dry on the hike to Marymere Falls.

spectacular view is from the eastern shores of Puget Sound, as you can see most of the major peaks strung out across the western horizon. Some mistaken reports aside, you cannot see Mt. Olympus from Puget Sound. Lesser peaks hide it from the east.

Put a beach hike down on your must-do list, but if you're like most residents, you'll probably never get around to doing it. Since most of the coastal strip of the national park does not have roads along it, you must be certain you want to make the long hike before setting out. You will have little choice but complete it once you start.

Two beach areas accessible by highway are extremely popular; they are **Kalaloch** and **Ruby Beach**, both off U.S. 101 just north of Queets. Camping is available at Kalaloch, if you're lucky enough to get there early in the day, or early on Fridays during the summer. The drive along this section is spectacular in itself because the trees that shelter the highway are so tall and so dense

A child hops across the small stream that tumbles over the cliff as Marymere Falls, a short hike from the south shore of Lake Crescent.

that the two-lane highway is dwarfed and looks almost as wide as a normal sidewalk. The National Park Service has found enough points of interest off the highway—such as gigantic trees—to give you excuses to mosey along rather than make miles.

In spite of the highway, resorts, and campgrounds along the Olympic coast, it still retains a wild quality that can easily make you feel a bit uneasy. The shipwrecks, the weather, the gloom of storms that seem to be either arriving or departing if they aren't overhead—all make you feel a bit insignificant.

And the history. Along here were Indian tribes with a highly developed art, as shown in the artifacts excavated from the Ozette village at Cape Alava. It was here that one of the most tragic love stories in Northwest history came to a bitter end. This is the story of Anna Petrovna.

In 1808, while Russia still held Alaska and nobody was certain how much more of the West Coast, a party was sent out from New Archangel (now Sitka) to find a site for a fort near the mouth of the Columbia River. The commander of the expedition was Nikolai Bulygin. His wife, Anna Petrovna Bulygina, traveled with him and a crew of 20 aboard a brig, *Saint Nicholas*.

One night in October, after trading along the route, they stopped at Destruction Island near the

The jumbled pile of logs and driftwood blown up on Dungeness Spit provides a picnic table for young hikers.

Strait of Juan de Fuca's entrance and set three anchors on the rocky bottom. But a strong sou'wester blew up and snapped the anchor cables, one by one, and by morning the brig was on the rocks for good.

They set up camp and tried to salvage everything of any value off the ship. But, before the day was over, they had a skirmish with the Quillayute Indians who lived nearby. Three Indians were killed in a dispute that apparently could have been settled by negotiation instead of violence. At any rate, the die was cast.

They stripped the ship of everything they could, threw the rest into the water to keep it away from the Indians, then struck out on foot for Grays Harbor to meet another party due there in December.

The Indians held councils and sent word all

Dungeness Spit, seven miles long and still growing, is the longest natural sandspit in the nation. A lighthouse at the tip is the goal of many hikers, who usually bring lunches along, and must bring drinking water.

along the coast of what the Russians had done. A trap was set for the Russians at the Hoh River, the first stream too deep to wade across. In the meantime, they harrassed the Russians with spears and stones along the route. The Russians reached the Hoh River in early November and began negotiations for renting dugouts to ferry them across.

The Indians agreed, then attacked when the Russians were in the middle of the stream. The canoe bearing Anna and a few others was captured and taken away. The Russians beat a retreat up the Hoh River, searching for a good campsite and a place to make a stand against the Indians. They met two chiefs who offered to sell them whale blubber and to sell Anna back to her husband. By this time Bulygin had relieved himself of command, since he was not a woodsman, and his replacement first demanded that they see Anna to be sure she was alive. The Indians brought her up the other side of the Hoh, and the chiefs demanded four guns in exchange for her. The new commander, Tarakanov, refused to part with the precious muskets, so the Indians took Anna away.

11

Clamming

Several times a year you'll see crowds of people on the ocean beaches intent on giving the impression they're trying to make the beaches look like Normandy after a mortar attack. If you're a native, you'll know there's a minus tide, and the clam diggers are out for the premium ingredient of clam chowder.

While there are minus-tide series throughout the year, one of the best times to head for the beach for clams is during the spring while it is still too cold for the less hardy diggers, and the out-of-staters haven't arrived yet in numbers.

And don't get excited if you think the diggers are ruining the beach by leaving unsightly holes and piles of sand. The next incoming tide will wipe it all clean, leaving the beach smooth and packed again.

Clamming is one of the bonuses of living near the ocean, and one of the least expensive methods of food gathering. All it takes is a shovel, or a so-called clam gun, and something to carry them in after you've dug them.

The limit is the first fifteen clams you dig, regardless of size or condition. It isn't quite like picking up a head of lettuce in a supermarket. Once you've hoisted one out of the sand, chances are it has been injured or killed, and there's nothing to be gained by returning them.

Razor clams live only a few inches below the surface of the sand with their necks sticking upward to take in the nutrients of the salt water. When the water recedes, they pull in their necks to sit out the tide change, and by doing so, leave a small pock mark in the sand, giving away their location.

If you can't find the pock marks, or dimples as some call them, try stamping or slapping your shovel on the sand. The vibration will startle them into squirting water up out of the sand, giving away their presence.

There are two main tools for digging: the clam shovel, which is a flat-bladed and short-handled shovel, and the clam gun, a metal tube at least four inches across. It is plunged down into the sand then extracted with the tube filled with the sand—and usually the clam.

When a clam's location is found, you must start the digging slightly seaward from it because when in danger, they start toward the safety of the water. And they can move! Although they are buried in the apparently hard-packed beach, their digging implements permit them to be somewhere else by the time you reach where you think they are.

Some prefer the gun, or tube, because it doesn't always require you to get down on your hands and knees, probing around in the hole in the wet sand. In fact, if you must keep a dignified countenance at all time, clam digging probably isn't your sport at all.

Digging is legal 24 hours a day (yes, some do dig by lantern) from October 1 to March 15, and from midnight to noon from March 16 to June 30. No digging is permitted between July through September to allow spawning.

A young angler works the surf on the Olympic Coast.

They were trapped in the forest through November, December and January, painfully making their way up the river knowing they would never meet the other party at Grays Harbor. Bulygin took over again, and they loaded aboard a dugout belonging to a friendly Indian they hired. He announced he would search for Anna on the way downriver. After much debate among the crew that remained alive, they finally agreed and captured two Indians, one a woman whose husband was a man of some stature in the tribe.

They waited eight days, then had a parley with the Makahs, who let Anna be seen—and she was a changed woman. She belonged to a chief who had treated her well. She was clean, had good clothes, and she refused to leave the Indians and return to her Russian husband and his crew. This almost destroyed Bulygin.

She offered them safety with the Indians until they could catch a boat back to Alaska. About half of the crew decided against it and took off down the Hoh in their dugout. But they struck a rock and lost their arms and ammunition. They were captured, and at least two of them were sold as slaves to other tribes.

The other captives were treated reasonably well and were scattered among various villages, where they lived through the spring and summer of 1809. But eventually the Indians began treating them simply as slaves, in part because their ships did not come.

Anna died that August, an apparent suicide, because her chief had sold her to another Indian who was described as such a barbarian that when she died, he had her body thrown into the forest instead of buried.

The crew was finally rescued in 1810 by a Boston brig, *Lydia*. Seven of the original 20 were dead, and others were bought by the Bostonians from as far away as the Columbia. Bulygin had died after Anna's death, but the others were made of hardier stuff.

Since the account of the Russians' experience was written by Tarakanov, who relieved Bulygin of his command, we cannot be certain of the accuracy of his version of Anna's last months. Whatever the true facts, Anna was the first white woman to visit the Olympic coast, and her story is one of the more tragic ones along the coast.

Storm Watching

Several years ago when it was first suggested to a beach resort community that they begin advertising winter storms as a tourist attraction, the chamber of commerce officers recoiled in horror, as though someone had recommended listing their sewage lagoon as a tourist attraction. At that time the beach towns considered themselves in competition with the California coast towns, or even Miami, and believed storms were a negative factor.

But gradually winter-storm watching forced itself upon the coastal towns, as inlanders began making reservations or simply showed up unannounced during foul weather. They brought their rain gear, rubber boots, and a supply of reading material. Now you'll often see beach resort areas advertising their winter storms and special winter rates.

Motels and cottages with fireplaces appear to have the edge on the market because there is nothing quite as cozy as a cabin or room with a crackling fireplace while rain and wind batter the windows. Hot drinks, warm and dry clothing for outside, assorted driftwood, and the possibility of finding Japanese glass fishing floats after the storm and tide recede are enough for many beach visitors' happiness.

Some of the most pleasant Sunday mornings we've had on the coast were going out after a storm and digging through all the flotsam left on the beach. Other than the usual supply of plastic bottles (why are boaters so messy?) and the other treasures such as the floats, we've found ourselves wading in a sea of foam left behind by the waves dashing against the beach, pink and gold in the morning sun.

On another morning outing we were startled by a school of anchovies committing mass suicide swimming directly to the beach and lying around us by the hundred, flipping madly about until they died. While our children tried desperately to get them back into the water, we saw the reason for their action: a harbor seal reared its head a few feet offshore, and we assumed the fish were trying to escape the hungry seal.

The coast from the mouth of the Columbia north offers open season on storm watching. Unfortunately, many motels along the Long Beach Peninsula have become isolated from the ocean by the buildup of sand dunes since the jetties were built at the Columbia estuary. But some of the newer motels are out far enough, or high enough, to provide a view of the ocean and breakers.

A prime area for winter activities is **Ocean Shores**, a resort complex on the north end of Grays Harbor. North of this area the broad sandy beaches give way to headlands and offshore rocks.

A number of motels and resorts are open year-round. Best of all, most offer reduced rates during the winter, and the crowds of summer are elsewhere skiing or sulking at home.

14

Nomenclature

When, at Kalama, you enter Washington Territory, your ears begin to be assailed by the most barbarous names imaginable. On your way to Olympia by rail you cross a river called the **Skookum-chuck**; your train stops at places named **Newaukum, Tumwater,** and **Toutle**; and if you seek further, you will hear of whole counties labeled **Wahkiakum,** or **Snohomish,** or **Kitsar (Kitsap),** or **Klikatat;** and **Cowlitz, Hookium,** and **Nenole-lops** greet and offend you. They complain in Olympia that Washington Territory gets but little immigration; but what wonder? What man, having the whole American continent to choose from, would willingly date his letters from the county of Snohomish, or bring up his children in the city of Nenole-lops? The village of Tumwater is, as I am ready to bear witness, very pretty indeed; but surely an emigrant would think twice before he established himself either there or at Toutle. Seattle is sufficiently barbarous; **Steilacoom** is no better; and I suspect that the Northern Pacific Railroad terminus has been fixed at Tacoma because it is one of the few places on Puget Sound whose name does not inspire horror and disgust.

Charles Nordhoff, 1874

A duck's eye view of Dungeness Spit shows how it curves along the shore of the Strait of Juan de Fuca.

The Strait

When a neighbor suggested we stay at a small—very small—resort on the Strait of Juan de Fuca, we assumed it couldn't be much because we had never heard of it before. You know the attitude: "If I don't know what you're talking about, you must be wrong."

Fortunately, we took their word for it and called for reservations, then mailed a deposit. When we arrived a few weeks later for a four-day stay, we stopped at a farmhouse, checked in, and were given a key with instructions on how to get there: Drive through the gate (and close it, please, so the cows won't get out), follow the narrow dirt road down through the field and timber, our cabin would be right on the beach.

We followed the directions and found a weathered, unpainted and obviously elderly cabin just off the beach with a big pile of wood behind complete with axe and chop block.

Although it wasn't much for looks, the interior was immaculate. It had a relatively large living room with a big stove in the far corner and a network of pipes running in and out of it. The bathroom was behind it, and another tiny room had a double bed in it. There was no electricity, but the cabin came equipped with a kerosene lamp and a kerosene lantern. It did have running water, and those pipes we saw running through the stove produced the hot water.

After staying in some five-star hotels around the country, having the advantages of room service, laundry, and excellent restaurants, one would think we might be a bit edgy about such primitive accommodations. But we loved it. While we were there, we commented often on how much bother modern homes are, and I pontificated about what the children call my "olden days" when we had no plumbing problems because we had no plumbing; when we had no fears and expenses of electricity because there was no electrical service closer than 12 miles away; when we didn't worry about water pipes freezing and bursting or pay a water bill because we had a cistern behind the house with pure rain water in it.

Yet, after four days we were ready to return to the modern amenities. We learned how little light kerosene lamps give off for night reading; how impatient one becomes in the morning while waiting for the water to heat; how much of a chore it is to chop firewood every day. In other words, we learned just how much time used to be spent simply in keeping basic necessities available.

Yet those four days were very pleasurable. We heard no automobiles. We spent most evenings sitting on the beach watching ships and fishing boats glide by. We were greeted nearly every morning by dense fog that gradually thinned, then burned off by noon. It was a pleasant addition to our memory bank.

Crabbing

Probably the nicest thing about catching your own crab (other than the obvious difference in price) is that Dungeness crabs are easier to catch than fish—after you've found where they live. They're pretty fast, but unlike the old chestnut about tickling a fish on the tummy to soothe it while you catch it, you don't have to resort to trickery.

Crabs usually live in eel grass, sometimes in kelp and seaweed beds. On a minus-tide when virtually all the water has left the beach, you can literally pick them up off the beach. Usually, however, you'll have to reach down into the water after them. They're quite fast, and what you may mistake for a shadow moving on the water can be a crab.

Some people use bamboo garden rakes to catch them. They get the crab entangled in the teeth, flip it over, and bring it to the surface. But most put on a pair of sturdy gloves and simply grab them, avoiding the claws that can deliver a crunching pinch. It is illegal to use anything sharp to penetrate the shells for the good reason that only male crabs can be taken. Males have narrow underbellies and a long triangular section of shell near the tail. Females have a wider underbelly and smaller triangular section. They must be returned to the sea.

The limit is six a day, and only males six inches across the shell in front of the points may be kept.

Heroes

Although I have never gone across any of the river bars and into the open ocean in a small boat, thousands do each year. They're welcome to it.

I say this after spending two days with the Coast Guard at Cape Disappointment near the mouth of the Columbia River. It is the second busiest Coast Guard station in America (Miami is first) in terms of rescues. In terms of danger, it ranks number one. Their attitude toward saving lives was succinctly summed up by a young lieutenant I went out with aboard a rescue boat. I asked him if there were any conditions under which they wouldn't go out.

"Not if there's a life involved," he replied.

History supports their attitude. They have sent boat crews out in the worst storms to hit the coast. They have lost men and boats trying to save the lives of commercial fishermen and others trapped on the ocean during those storms. Cape Disappointment is the training base for rescue operations because it is located on the stormiest stretch of coast in America. Almost every week they can find seas and surf sufficiently heavy to show the young sailors how to make rescues under the most dangerous conditions.

Unfortunately, the Coast Guart isn't empowered to tell pleasure boaters to stay home when conditions are too dangerous. They would save a lot of lives—including their own—if they could enforce common sense. But all the Coast Guard can do is be prepared to haul people out of the water when their boats overturn or tow boats back to safety when they lose power or are swamped.

My first experience with the Coast Guard came during a weekend at Long Beach. Early one morning I ventured out on the north jetty to take some photos of the tail end of a storm that was throwing waves over the jetty. But when I got there, I found a crowd of people watching a troller that had missed the channel across the Columbia River bar and was aground about 200 feet north of the jetty. A Coast Guard crew arrived soon in a jeep, and a bleary-eyed petty officer said they would get a surfboat and helicopter out as soon as they could.

A group of commercial fishermen were gathered around muttering among themselves about the poor service. They became openly hostile toward the petty officer and his small crew. About a week earlier the Coast Guard had rescued a Russian fisherman who had a ruptured appendix from a factory ship, and the fishermen were bitter about it. They considered the Russians not only our political enemies, but also fish thieves. They didn't think the Coast Guard should help them, even to save a life.

The petty officer took the abuse silently. I asked him how long it had been since he had been to bed. "Two days," he replied. During the storm every man on the base had been busy with rescue operations. Every boat, every jeep, every helicopter was in constant use. They had to make rescues where lives seemed in jeopardy, leaving property damage rescues until later. Since the skipper of the commercial boat stuck in the sand had simply climbed down and walked to the beach, this boat would have to wait.

About an hour later a helicopter arrived, then a small surfboat. The surfboat pulled in as close as it could, bobbing wildly about while the men from the jeep got a line from the beached boat to the surfboat with the aid of the helicopter.

Then the helicopter left for another rescue operation. The surfboat couldn't budge the fishing boat because the tide was going out. They had to give up and go away, leaving the jeep crew there to take the wrath of the fishermen.

The incident always bothered me, but it wasn't until about eight years later that I had a chance to go out with the Coast Guard and see how they operate. Along with firemen, they are among our last authentic heroes. They function only to save lives and property. Unlike the television heroes, they do not shoot the bad guys. They do not get involved in barroom brawls while going about their duties. They do not shoot down airplanes, sink ships, bombard shore installations, or fire torpedoes. Thus, you will never see a television series about them.

They know from personal experience how it feels to be aboard a boat that has flipped completely over in the surf. They know about how long they will have to hold their breath, strapped to the boat, before it rights itself again. They know how long those seconds are under water, how noisy it is under there and how frightening.

They know how ungrateful most people are whose lives they save after they have done something stupid. "Why'd it take you so long?" "I'll have a word with my congressman about this," and so forth.

The pity is that they are never treated like the heroes they really are. It is their job, we think, and why should they be praised for doing that job, even if it involves considerable risk on their part?

I once spent a weekend with the Cape Disappointment coast guardsmen writing a story about the training programs conducted there. The cape was chosen for coxswain and rescue training because they can almost always promise heavy seas and crashing surf to show trainees what to expect while making rescues in stormy weather.

I went aboard one of the larger boats, about 50 feet, with the station commander. While the smaller motor lifeboats (surfboats is the common and apt description of them) worked into the surf like a maniac from Maui, we stood off outside the breakers watching them practice rescues. The heavy sea was simply lifting our boat, then dropping it down into the troughs, and we weren't getting wet.

But along came one of those rogue waves every seaman knows, and instead of the boat rising over the crest, the crest rose over us. The wave knocked two of us off our feet, and I fell against the station commander, almost knocking him down, too. It was a small thing, but a reminder of what to expect out there.

In the station, which is tucked around behind the cape away from the heavy seas, there is a story of the greatest disaster to hit the station, posted where the men and visitors alike are reminded constantly of their mission.

While Coast Guard rescues in foul weather are routine, the worst experience on record was in January, 1961, when small-craft warnings had been flying daily for two weeks, flags stiff in the gales as if starched into position.

Men who fish for a living tend to get restless during such periods, and two brothers, Bert and Stanley Bergman, were no exception. They had

weathered storms before in their 40-foot boat, so they went out into the heavy weather to tend their crab pots north of the Columbia River bar near Peacock Spit. While they were going about their way of life, the heavy seas broke their rudder. They called the Coast Guard for assistance.

Naturally the Coast Guard responded immediately with a 40-footer from Point Adams on the Oregon side of the river. The three crew members found the Bergman's boat, the *Mermaid*, and got a towline on her. But the seas were so heavy by then they were unable to make any headway. They radioed for more help, and the 52-foot *Triumph* came out. In the meantime a 36-footer had joined the 40-footer, and when the *Triumph* arrived, both smaller ones headed in for safety. The seas were simply too much for them.

But on the way in, the 40-footer capsized, and all three crew members went over into the sea. The 36-footer was able to pick them up, and they went back to base.

By dark the storm had reached its peak with winds at a steady 75 knots, gusting off the gauges. The seas were running 60 feet high, and the wind broke off all radio antennas. The last message to reach shore stations was when the 40-footer capsized. Those on shore could only hope and wait.

Then the 213-foot cutter *Yacona* left port at Astoria to join in the rescue, and as soon as they were under way, the captain told the crew they must assume that "all boats were down and the men in the water."

Planes armed with giant flares were sent down from Port Angeles, and another cutter got under way far down the Oregon coast at Coos Bay. There was little hope it could fight the seas and arrive in time to be of any help.

The men aboard the *Yacona* were taking the worst beating of their careers. Walls of water roaring over the flying bridge 42 feet above the waterline were knocking them off their feet, and spray was cutting their faces like sand. Fire extinguishers were ripped from their hangers and crashed wildly around the ship. Fire hoses snapped loose and snaked and whipped around, almost crippling several sailors.

Suddenly, in the terror and storm, a

searchlight from the *Yacona* picked out a ghostly scene that survivors still see in their dreams. Off the port bow, rising to the crest of the waves, then plunging down and out of sight into the troughs, were the *Mermaid* and the *Triiumph*.

The men on the cutter could see four of the five *Triumph* crewmen on deck as she turned about in the storm to put another towline on the *Mermaid*. One of the Bergman brothers was clinging to the bow, waiting for the line from the coast guardsmen.

The *Yacona* crew thought they saw a light in the water off the starboard beam and turned toward it since their first responsibility was to someone in the water.

Just after they turned, the *Triumph* capsized. Still another Coast Guard boat in the area dashed over to try to get a towline on the *Mormaid*. But before they could, the *Mermaid* also capsized and disappeared.

The only survivor of the *Triumph* was Gordon Higgins, who was below checking the engines when she went over. When she righted herself, Higgins went up to the deck and hung on until she ran aground on Benson Beach near North Head. There he was found by beach patrols.

The 36-footer that had made the last attempt to save the *Mermaid* was damaged, and the coxswain limped her out to the Lightship *Columbia*, perpetually anchored at the bar, and got his crew aboard safely. During the night his boat sank.

The night's toll: seven men and four vessels. Only one body was recovered, the coxswain of the *Triumph*. A door off the *Triumph* was washed up on the beach later.

Much of the town of Oysterville has been preserved by federal and state historic landmark status, including the R.H. Espy home.

20

Long Beach

Several years ago when our children were still small enough to be crammed into a small car, we were traveling the Oregon coast to research a book and ended our trip at Brookings. We had three more days of vacation remaining and planned to use them on the return trip north to Washington. But every motel on the Oregon coast was suddenly filled, and we weren't carrying our camping gear. We darted in and out of every town along the coast, tired and hungry and dreading a long drive all the way home to Seattle from the California border.

About 10:30 that night we arrived in Long Beach and decided to make one more try. We stopped at a motel and were told they were full. But, wonder of wonders, the clerk said she'd be happy to make some calls and see if she couldn't find a place for us. She called several places, then found one with enough room for us. We drove over and found not only enough space for us, but also that room was in a two-story unit of an older motel that apparently had been something else when it was built. We were so delighted with it—and its kitchen—that we decided to stay two extra nights.

On other trips to the peninsula, we have stayed in new motels and old ones and have never been disappointed. In the vernacular of now, the Long Beach Peninsula has a laid-back atmosphere. It is a marvelous blending of tourism and working

people—the fishermen and farmers. But we've never managed to get one of our trips down there to coincide with the cranberry harvest.

The local newspaper publishes one of the best tourist-information editions in the state and thoughtfully includes a map showing where all the shipwrecks have occurred since records were started. It is for good reason that the area both north and south of the Columbia estuary has been called "The Graveyard of the Pacific." Some bits and pieces of the wrecks can still be seen at low tide, and hardly a winter passes that beachcombers don't find flotsam from either a shipwreck or material torn loose from barges or container ships off the coast.

The area has a fascinating history. During the years of intense salmon fishing one of the most popular methods of catching them was by using horses to wade out into the shallows and tow nets between them. Fish traps were pounded into the water, and for a time the small town of Chinook had the highest per capita income of any town in the country.

Ilwaco is still a major fishing port, although much of its activity now is from charter salmon fishing instead of commercial. Like other charter boat towns, the motel owners operate on a different schedule than those along freeways. They get up very early—3 or 4 a.m.—to be sure everyone scheduled on the charter trips are up and out. Most restaurants will provide box lunches for the fishermen and lots of strong coffee. And pills to combat seasickness are sold everywhere.

The town of Long Beach has dozens of motels, it seems, plus an amusement park with rides and a museum of wierd artifacts gathered from around the world. Its restaurants offer excellent seafood, and the grocery stores' shelves have an abundance of snack, party, and picnic items.

North up the peninsula are small towns with more motels, campgrounds, and farms. Perhaps the most famous small town is Oysterville, part of which is now on the National Register of Historic Sites. It and another charming town, Nahcotta, are on the Willapa Bay side of the peninsula where the

water is more calm and the shore stretches out across mudflats at low tide.

At the very tip of the peninsula is Ledbetter Point, an undeveloped area of vast, tall sand dunes, pine, and underbrush. Part of it is a national wildlife refuge and part is a state park.

Numerous artists and artisans have made their homes on the peninsula, and galleries show their work. Other attractions include the Lewis and Clark Interpretive Center in Fort Canby State Park, the Willapa Bay Wildlife Refuge, and the 28 miles of beach over which you can drive your car at low tide. But be forewarned: Beach driving may be fun, but it is not good for your car and is potentially dangerous for pedestrians. It is better to walk on the beach or rent a saddle horse. You can't build a sandcastle or beachcomb from your car.

Beaches are probably the best babysitter in the state, and only hunger seems to drive the children inside.

Smelt

Just after I got my first newspaper job in
Washington, after serving an apprenticeship in
Seaside, Oregon, the managing editor of the paper,
the *Longview Daily News*, told me to prepare
myself for some fun when the smelt began running.
Well, I'd been through all that before as a Boy
Scout in Missouri holding the sack on a snipe hunt.

The editor, Carlton Moore, saw my skeptical
look and just told me to wait. When they began
running a few weeks later that March, I became a
believer. Never have I seen such wild activity as on
the banks of the Cowlitz River when the tiny, oily
fish began migrating upstream to spawn. People of
all ages were out there working in teams. One
manipulated the net on the end of a 15-foot-long
pole, and the other unloaded the net when it was
swung to shore. It wasn't unusual for poles to bang
against each other or for nets to become entangled.
There were stories of fisticuffs on the banks of the
Cowlitz, although I never saw any.

Smelt dippers come from all over the state
when the fish are running and, after they get the
hang of it, can get their limit of 20 pounds per
person (a day) in a short time. They soon learn that
since the fish are headed upstream, it is best to
start the swing with the net as far upstream as they
can reach; let the net move across the bottom as
the current pushes it downstream, while
(hopefully) the smelt swim into the net and become
entangled.

Since there is a stiff fine for going over the
limit, it is wise to be sure you don't get carried
away with the sport and forget the limit until
your arms are sore. One way to keep reminding
yourself is to put the smelt in 2½-gallon pails.
Each pail full of smelt weights exactly 20 pounds.
One pail, one limit.

While I was living in Longview, it was my duty
one weekend to cover the annual smelt-eating
contest held at the Eagle's in Kelso. I can't
remember how many the winner ate that year in
the allotted time, and I don't really care any more.
All I remember is watching the young man who
won lurch outside during the contest with a judge
on his heels to be sure he didn't "dispose" of what
he'd already eaten. The young man took several

deep breaths, wandered aimlessly around the
parking lot a few minutes, then went back inside to
win the contest. Although it left me with a notable
lack of interest in eating smelt thereafter, the story
did win me a bonus at work when I called the
contestants "abdominable showmen."

Smelt are totally unpredictable fish. While
they may make their appearance most of the time
in the Cowlitz, and seem to favor it over other
Columbia tributaries, there are years when they
don't spawn in it at all. They may go on up to the
Lewis River, or still farther to the Sandy River in
Oregon. Or they may divide their forces into all
three rivers, or they may hardly make a showing
anywhere in the Columbia.

Smelt aren't limited to the tributaries of the
Columbia. They come up numerous other rivers of
the state to spawn. A healthy run moves down
Hood Canal nearly every year. Others go up the
Swinomish Slough past La Conner each February
and March.

LaConner holds an annual Smelt Derby
sponsored by the local Rotary Club with prizes for
the largest smelt caught according to ages of the
contestants, plus the largest herring, bullhead, cod,
flounder, and whatever else happens to find its way
into the slough. Here smelt are caught by jigging
rather than dipping. This is accomplished with
nine small hooks tied on a line with a sinker on the
bottom, jigged up and down in the slough to snag
the fish.

Now that you know how to catch them two
ways, how do you cook them? Some people cook
them whole, since their internal organs have
usually been consumed by their peculiar digestive
system. This is because they are on their way to
spawn and don't eat after leaving the ocean, so
their internal organs disappear. The only thing
inside them would be the sperm and eggs, but
cooking removes all traces of them.

Most people don't take to this and prefer
cleaning them first. This is a simple chore
accomplished with a filleting knife by splitting the
belly all the way up (or down), removing the head,
and cleaning out the offal. Roll them in a mixture
of flour and cornmeal, fry them until crisp, and
that's all there is to it.

Fog

Fog, one must admit, does have its disadvantages. It makes driving and flying hazardous, small-boating almost impossible, and turns scenery that is spectacular on sunny days into a blank, gray nothing. Nobody, it seems, can think of anything good to say about fog.

Yet, since the entire nation at one time or another is subjected to fog, perhaps it would be better to think of it as something that not only can be endured, but enjoyed—like thunderstorms, droughts, and minus 32 degrees Fahrenheit.

Fog does have its own beauty. It both mutes and emphasizes the landscape, giving it rose and lavender tints that no clear, cloudless day can match. It turns an evening and a pond into a scene no Old Master could match. It changes sunlight into thin, delicate streamers reaching to the forest floor to illuminate a vine or a berry one might otherwise overlook. And a morning that an hour ago was rather bleak now is soft, subtle, and memorable.

26

THE COLUMBIA

AN indication that you have lived in one place too long (or maybe have simply lived too long) is when you spend more time talking about what was than what is or can be. It is tempting to dwell too much on the past when talking about the Columbia River. Before the industrial revolution arrived in the Northwest, the Columbia was a force of nature. It flowed swiftly over rapids and low waterfalls. Each year it was virtually filled with salmon. The sturgeon, a prehistoric giant, grew to monster proportions. Nobody living along the river had to go hungry, if they didn't mind a diet of fish.

Now only two stretches of the river remain free flowing: one through the Hanford Atomic Reservation in eastern Washington and the other from Bonneville Dam to the sea. Otherwise, we could never be certain any more that it actually is a river. The only hint of wildness remaining are the steep canyons along the river and a few side streams and waterfalls tumbling into the Columbia Gorge. Below Bonneville the river is controlled by hundreds of pile dikes and dredged almost constantly to keep the shipping channel at least 40 feet deep to permit ships to come all the way up to Portland.

There is little use in lamenting what has happened to the Columbia. Yet we can feel cheated that we weren't around when the dams were only plans, when Indians gathered on rickety platforms to hook or net salmon over Celilo Falls, when the Cascades were more than a spot on an old map, when the river had sound to it.

Sometimes motorists on Highway 830 along the Columbia River are startled to see an ocean-going ship materialize beside them in the river. Ships go upriver as far as Portland and Vancouver.

Lewis and Clark Country

Most of them were ill, some so weak they could only lie in the bottom of the canoes as they shot the rapids on the Snake River. During portages around the worst stretches, the ill had to be helped up to the barren shores of eastern Washington. The local Indians weren't as friendly and helpful as the Nez Perce had been after the hard crossing over the Bitteroots, and the closer they got to the coast, the more unfriendly and thieving the Indians became.

But the Lewis and Clark party pressed on, down the Columbia River Gorge in that cold and rainy October of 1805, stopping to portage around Celilo Falls, the Dalles, the Cascades. They became so infested with vermin that they sometimes traveled nude.

It rained most of the way through the gorge and down to the ocean. They noted the fluctuations of the lower river as the tides rose and fell, almost lost some canoes when a storm blew up one night and smashed them against rocks. They were continually wet and cold, and in spite of the famous "Oh, Joy!" when they mistakenly thought they were at the coast, they kept moving to the west. They finally reached land's end near the present town of Chinook, Washington, established a camp and began looking for winter quarters. They were unable to find adequate shelter or a good source of deer and elk, and the Chinooks were not especially friendly. So they moved across the river and eventually set up camp at what is now **Fort Clatsop National Monument**, southwest of Astoria.

The Lewis and Clark Expedition is firmly stuck in the national conscience as one of our greatest undertakings. They were given a tough job—an expedition into the unknown—and they went out and did it with no excuses, no complaining, and apparently no regrets. They are authentic heroes, and their exploits are as well appreciated in other parts of the world as in America.

Their route from the Snake to the Pacific has been changed beyond their wildest dreams. The place they built canoes for the Snake and Columbia passage is barely in existence across the

31

Clearwater River from a sawmill in Idaho. The entire Snake River of their route is a series of slackwater pools behind dams. The barren banks now are checkerboarded with wheat farms and orchards. There is no moving water on the Columbia until just past Celilo Falls, where Bonneville Dam stands. Although the water from there to the ocean is free of dams, cities have been built along its banks, plus pile dikes, earth-fill dikes with roads on them, bridges, a nuclear-power plant. The river is always busy with tugs, barges, log booms, ships, and pleasure boats.

This isn't to say the river is less beautiful now than then (except in the Columbia Gorge, where one wishes they had left one or two of the sets of rapids for aesthetics if no other reason). The river still has a form of beauty that is different than the old wild river days. One of my favorite scenes on the Snake River was early one morning when I was driving with a photographer up to Lions Ferry State Park. Our first view of the Snake was a still pool with small islets and peninsulas jutting into the water, perfectly reflecting the landscape and

sky, a touch of fog hanging here and there. By the time we crossed that arching bridge over the Snake, which stood over the Columbia at Vantage before Wanapum Dam and I-90 were built, the wind was stirring and the scene was totally different, not nearly so interesting.

The Snake is still relatively inaccessible between Clarkson and Pasco. Although there are highways and county roads crossing the Snake at intervals, there still are long stretches with no road access.

It is a different matter on the Columbia. There are highways on both sides of the river—a four-lane freeway on the Oregon side—all the way down to the estuary. At no other place in the state is the transition from the arid eastern Washington to the humid, rainy western Washington more apparent than along the Columbia Gorge. Yet we have

This replica of England's Stonehenge at Maryhill was built by Samuel Hill near the Maryhill Museum as a memorial to World War I casualties.

33

driven the route a number of times and cannot spot the exact place where desert and rain forest meet. The merger is so gradual it is almost imperceptible.

Perhaps more than any other place in the state, one is aware of waterfalls while traveling through the gorge. They can be seen on both sides of the river all the way through. Occasionally when one tops a hill, one of the three Guardians of the Columbia—Mt. Adams, Mt. St. Helens, and Mt. Hood in Oregon—will suddenly appear unexpectedly looming over the treetops and the lower mountains. Part of the Klickitat Indian legend, from which the Guardians story comes, is preserved in the naming of the Bridge of the Gods near Bonneville Dam.

The legend:

The god Tyhee Saghalie had two sons, Wy'east, leader of the Multnomah tribe south of the Columbia, and Klickitat, leader of the tribe bearing his name north of the Columbia. In order for them to visit back and forth, Tyhee Saghalie built a stone bridge across the river. Then, in return for the gift of fire, Tyhee Saghalie transformed an ugly crone, Loowit, into a beautiful maiden. Both sons fell in love with her and began fighting for her hand in marriage.

In anger and sadness Tyhee Saghalie destroyed the bridge and killed both his sons and Loowit. But because he loved all three and wanted them to be immortal, he changed them into mountains. Wy'east became Mt. Hood, Klickitat became Mt. Adams, and because Loowit was so beautiful, she became the graceful Mt. St. Helens.

Inquisitive white men soon began looking for some basis for the legend in fact. Lewis and Clark recorded they saw submerged tree trunks beneath the river near the Cascades. After the radio-carbon dating method was perfected, some of those submerged trees were hauled out of the river before the Bonneville Dam was built. Their burial was placed about 700 years ago, which gave some credence to an Indian's statement that the bridge existed there "about 20 squaws ago," or about 600 years ago, since the average life span for Indians then was about 30 years.

Today it is believed that a massive landslide, perhaps triggered by an earthquake, tumbled part of Table Mountain into the Columbia and created an earth-and-rock dam that temporarily blocked the river. When the river broke through, the Cascades were created.

The first major city along the Columbia is Vancouver, too often lumped into one urban area with Portland, but a distinct city with a major share in Northwest history. It was here that the Hudson's Bay Co. had a big fort and the famous factor, Dr. John McLoughlin, lived. Hudson's Bay believed he was much too friendly to American settlers on what the British then considered their territory. He was as much responsible for the Oregon Country becoming American as anyone else, although in an indirect way. Simply by helping new arrivals, he encouraged settlement of the Northwest by people other than trappers.

The **Fort Vancouver National Historic Site** was built on the river plain below the city with an interpretive center and the restored fort, which has a stockade, bakery, smithy, fur warehouse, and other buildings used by the Hudson's Bay people. Also nearby are remains of the U.S. Army fort where its most famous officer, Ulysses S. Grant, was stationed for awhile. Although Grant had a definite drinking problem at the time, the captain who became general and President managed to have a garden (even officers worked in those days). And a building erected in 1849—the oldest building in Vancouver—has been named the **U.S. Grant Museum**. About the only thing directly related to Grant is some furniture, but it also houses a collection of Indian artifacts, antique glassware, and china. It originally was a log building, but it since has been covered with siding.

Also of interest in Vancouver is the **Clark County Historical Museum** at 16th and Main. It has a fully stocked pioneer doctor's office, complete with a display of drugs, plus a stocked 1890s store and an antique printing press.

From Vancouver onward, the Columbia begins spreading out in both directions because the mountains have been left behind. There are hundreds of sloughs and small islands, many with giant log booms tied to them awaiting their turn at the mills scattered along the river. The river is so wide that the flow is difficult to detect from the bank, but it does exist and is subject to the rise and fall of the tides all the way back to Bonneville

34

Dam. Tugs and towboats must work with tide tables, and sometimes the river current is so strong that a tug with a heavy tow will have to pull over to the bank and tie up until the tide changes. Ocean-going ships cruise up and down the river, calling on Portland and grain elevators at Kalama and Longview.

Interstate 5 stays in sight of the river most of the way to Longview, but the best river views are from Washington 4, which runs from Longveiw to the ocean on the Washington side of the river. In many places it clings to cliffs directly over the river, and it sometimes startles motorists to see a huge ocean-going vessel apparently coming right through the trees toward them. One of my most

memorable scenes was standing in the fog at the small town of **Stella** and suddenly seeing a big freighter materialize out of the fog without a sound. It had been anchored there waiting for the fog to lift, and its sudden appearance gave momentary credence to the legend of the Flying Dutchman.

In this same area are more log booms tied to ancient piling in the sloughs, and it is always interesting to stop and walk down to the piling in the spring when wildflowers and even small willows are growing out of them. Sometimes a log boom will

Puget Island's series of sloughs give many residents one- and two-boat garages, and if they want, they can attend the First Lutheran Church by boat.

Houses and fishing boats line the bank of Skamokawa Creek in the picturesque town of the same name on the Columbia River.

be left in one place for several years before its turn comes at the paper mills, and they, too, will be sprouting a crop of weeds, willows, or even tiny Douglas fir.

Just west of Stella the road drops back down to the river again, and it is a rare day when there won't be at least a dozen fishermen taking it easy while catching dinner. This stretch of beach near the Cowlitz-Wahkiakum County line is often called "Social Security Beach," in honor of the large population of retired men who fish there. They cast out into the river, securely anchor their rods in the sand with stones or blocks of wood, hang a bell on the pole, then go to their vehicle or gather around a community fire and listen for the bells to toll. Even in the foulest of weather, there will almost always be at least two or three fishermen there, sitting in the comfort of their campers and watching their rods.

The next town is **Cathlamet**, county seat of Wahkiakum County and one of those historical towns that never took itself too seriously until the combination of the Bicentennial and *Roots* made us all aware of the value of our past. Cathlamet has been busy recently sprucing itself up, restoring an old hotel and restaurant, repairing a historic church, and establishing a group of community players to perform plays during the summer season.

Many northern Europeans settled in this area around the turn of the century, and several from Switzerland started farms on Puget Island, which is reached from Cathlamet by bridge at the end of the main street. Puget Island is mainly dairy farming land and is surrounded by a system of dikes on which roads have been built. It is also laced with long, narrow sloughs where residents have built boathouses that look like garages. Several commercial fishermen live on the island and keep their gillnet boats tied up behind their houses.

A small ferry runs from the south side of the island to the small town of Westport, Oregon, one of the few remaining ferries on the Columbia. It is the only crossing between Longview and the Astoria-Megler Bridge near the river's mouth.

The highway swings back inland from Cathlamet and goes past the **Columbian White-tailed Deer National Wildlife Refuge**, where you'll see the deer grazing peacefully beside dairy cattle. A sign just beyond a bridge leads one back toward the river and along a county road that goes through the refuge, offering a better view of the endangered species thriving in the refuge. The road reaches the main highway again near the picturesque town of Skamokawa.

Skamokawa is built where Skamokawa Creek enters the Columbia, and houses line both sides of the creek and part of the river. Some have small green lawns on the bank, and nearly all have a boat dock of some kind. One of the few remaining steamboat docks on the river still stands at Skamokawa, and perched on a hill just above the bridge that crosses the creek is one of the Lower Columbia landmarks, Redmen Hall.

There once was a fraternal organization that had Redmen Halls around the country; the organization died, and the hall in Skamokawa is one of the few still standing. A Chicago businessman named Pierre Pype moved to Skamokawa and immediately went about restoring Redmen Hall. Naturally the local wags call it the Pype Dream.

Although the climate is mild and wet, often foggy in this area with little snow, during the winter one can almost always expect snow on the top of K-M Hill between Skamokawa and Grays River, which isn't much over 1,000 feet.

Grays River sits beside the river of the same name, another picturesque old town with a couple of stores, post office, tavern, and abandoned creamery. And just beyond town, about three curves on the twisting highway, is Grays River Covered Bridge, the last such bridge in use in the state. There are others built by railroads, but this is the last in use for automobile traffic.

Out of the one-store town of **Rosburg** is a side trip that every Lower Columbia visitor should make: the drive down to the Columbia River towns of **Altoona** and **Pillar Rock**. These towns were isolated for more than half a century and reached

only by river. Both were salmon-fishing towns with canneries built out over the river on piling. Both are still inhabited, but many of the old buildings are gradually falling into the river. There are no other towns in the state like them, and fewer anywhere in the state more picturesque.

The road down to them swings around Grays Bay, where the Grays River empties into the Columbia, and narrow side roads lead up small valleys past farms and summer homes. My wife's Finnish relatives settled in one of these valleys, **Eden Valley on Crooked Creek**, and they remember how the sail-powered fishing fleet would

Although Altoona is a shadow of its former use as a cannery town, the Columbia River village is still inhabited.

38

come into the bay in the evening, pretty as butterflies, and the men would tie them up, then go home up Crooked Creek in rowboats. For decades a small waiting room for steamboats sat on the bank beneath the Crooked Creek bridge, a tiny cabin with crumbling dock just pleading for historical preservation status. The last time we were there, the building was gone.

On the opposite, or west, side of Grays Bay is **Frankfort**, one of the few ghost towns of southwest Washington. It is reached by boat or by hiking through Crown Zellerbach land. You must get permission from the company to cross their land. Check at the office on the outskirts of Cathlamet.

Frankfort is an example of crossing a bridge before you get to it. It was born when railroad backers were certain they would get theirs built along the Washington side of the river before the Oregon railroad was completed. But through a series of maneuvers and mistakes, the Oregon line went to Astoria, ending any hopes for the Washington line.

Families used the homes, some quite elegant, for decades afterward as summer homes. For years the homes were safe and the rare visitor would find them completely equipped with furniture, curtains on the windows, china and silver. One had a fine piano in it.

When we visited the town in the mid-1960s, the piano had been smashed into splinters, no windows remained on the houses, all furniture of any value had been taken, and the houses were gradually rotting from the wet climate. An elderly bachelor lived alone there for many years, and after he left, commercial fishermen kept one or two of the smaller houses in good shape to sit out the tides or hole up there in case of a storm.

After swinging back away from the river through the small town of **Naselle**, Washington 401 returns to the river at the site of **Knappton**, where another major salmon cannery once stood. All that remains now are the rows of snaggled piling stubs, although only a few short years ago three or four buildings still stood on them, including the quarantine quarters where the imported Chinese laborers were kept for several days on their arrival.

The river is more than four miles wide at this point, and it is easy to understand why, in foul weather that obscured the far shore, Lewis and Clark believed they were at the ocean. During heavy weather the waves pound the beach, and there is a salty tang to the air as well as the water. Just beyond the Astoria-Megler toll bridge, the river widens again until at **Ilwaco** it is more than eight miles across, making it virtually impossible to pinpoint the place the ocean begins.

In the finest weather you can look back up the Columbia and see Mt. St. Helens and across the river to Saddle Mountain and beyond. In the worst rainy, foggy weather the area takes on an almost claustrophobic atmosphere, and in spite of the bridges and highways and dikes, there is the feeling of raw nature. It is such times that make motel visits a pleasure. A roaring fire, coffee perking in the kitchen, wind and rain pounding outside, and you're inside cozy and warm.

To complete the Lewis and Clark route, you should drive out to Cape Disappointment from Ilwaco through Fort Canby and up to the new **Lewis and Clark Interpretive Center** high on the cape overlooking the ocean. It is undoubtedly the best view of the coast in the whole area.

THE CASCADES

WHEN I drove over the Cascades for the first time that September afternoon in 1959, I was dutifully unimpressed. After all, I had worked on ranches in Colorado at elevations more than 8,000 feet, and here I was crossing a pass 3,000 feet lower. There were something like a dozen or more peaks higher than 14,000 feet in Colorado, while Washington had only Mt. Rainier in that category.

It was several months before I learned that the Cascades are as exciting and as varied as the Colorado Rockies, even though they are lower. The Cascades have caused me to make all kinds of vows, few of which I've kept. Among them are hiking the Pacific Crest Trail from Canada to the Columbia. I once planned to climb every Cascade volcano—Mt. Rainier, Mt. St. Helens, Mt. Adams, and Mt. Baker. I haven't climbed any.

No matter. Even if I don't spend a lot of time in them anymore, I'd rather have them there than the featureless horizon of the Great Planes or the series of humps we called mountains back in the Ozarks.

The Forest Service lookout on Nason Ridge near Stevens Pass is a popular destination for both hikers and horseback riders.

Three Passes

Sometimes when the landscape is obscured by rain and everything is that combination of gray and green unique to the Northwest, it is easy to imagine this part of the country before the white man came with his technology to level the timber and rearrange the hills and watercourses. At these times the landscape looks almost as though the processes of creation are still at work. The journals of Lewis and Clark, the accounts of James Gilchrist Swan, the combination travel writing and philosophical musings of Theodore Winthrop all take on an immediacy unlike most historical sources.

It is new country. The Civil War had been fought before the land was really settled, and early writers such as Winthrop, whose *The Canoe and the Saddle* was the first book written about the Northwest, held high hopes for this last corner. Winthrop especially believed the scenery itself—the awesome mountains and valleys and streams and islands in the inland sea—would have a positive effect on those who settled here. He found some evidence that his belief, or hope, would bear

Liberty Bell looms above the North Cascades Highway and Washington Pass.

fruit when he visited the Oregon Trail veteran, Jesse Applegate, who owned a large library in the wilderness of southern Oregon.

Washington was a bit more raw, he found. He had an incredibly difficult time crossing the Cascades with an Indian guide, and during that crossing in 1853 he encountered one of the worst federal boondoggles in the Northwest's young history. It was the large party—240 men—under the command of Capt. George Brinton McClellan sent to the Northwest supposedly to find a pass through the Cascades for a transcontinental railroad.

But there was a catch. Jefferson Davis was Secretary of War in those barely pre-Civil War days, and he didn't want the transcontinental railroad to go any farther than a general plan. He wanted a confederacy of southern slave states and did not want the powerful northern states united with this part of the country by a railroad. So his orders to McClellan were negative. He didn't want McClellan looking too hard for a crossing of the Cascades and ordered McClellan to report directly to him on his progress, or lack of it.

Winthrop encountered McClellan after the latter had spent some time at Fort Vancouver, where he had noted with disdain that an officer named Ulysses S. Grant was so impoverished that he had his own garden. McClellan didn't like Grant then, and he liked him even less as time went on and Grant began winning battles in the Civil War.

McClellan moved his army of soldiers and surveyors—and only three hunters to feed that large crew—north from Fort Vancouver, east around Mt. Adams, and cautiously along the eastern edge of the Cascades. Of course he never found a pass, even though Indians had for centuries crossed the Cascades at the major modern crossings.

Territorial Governor Isaac Ingalls Stevens knew better and made it a point to prove that McClellan was both wrong and committing a big boondoggle. He went past Chinook Pass, White Pass, Cowlitz Pass, Carleton Pass, Hart's Pass, Cascade Pass, Cispus Pass, and Twisp Pass. And he missed Stevens Pass and Snoqualmie Pass.

As the historian Robert Cantwell wrote in *The Hidden Northwest*, "An observer bearing a less

distinguished name might well have been dismissed as crazy for returning a report so obviously at variance with the facts."

For his part, Governor Stevens was so enraged that he sent an aide, Abiel Tinkham, over Snoqualmie Pass in midwinter, first from east to west, then back over it again.

Today, of course, the Cascades are threaded with highways and railroads crossing at low spots. The elusive **Snoqualmie Pass,** deemed too difficult by McClellan, now has a four-lane interstate highway across it. The summit with its snow McClellan so feared (or said he did) is one of Seattle's favorite playgrounds with a total of four ski resorts.

Still, in spite of the four lanes of traffic, a drive over Snoqualmie is a journey through some of the best scenery in the Cascades. One drives east past **North Bend;** the massive Mt. Si broods silently above town. The valley beyond North Bend lies flat beneath the mountains, then climbs along the flanks of the mountains, over clear and busy streams, up into low clouds, over Denny Creek, around a series of long curves and finally up the modest grade to the summit.

One of the best drives in the state lets you see the country McClellan missed because of the peculiar orders from the 1850s' equivalent of the Pentagon. It makes for a long day behind the wheel, but it is possible to drive around a loop and cross both Snoqualmie and Stevens Passes, with either **Swauk** or **Blewett Pass** thrown in as a bonus. Another bonus is swinging down off the main route a few miles to Leavenworth.

The route is I-90 east over Snoqualmie Pass to **Cle Elum,** the old coal mining town with pleasant cafes, one or two of which are exceptionally old with fancy carved-wood bars, high ceilings, and decorations more likely to be found in Wyoming than Washington.

From Cle Elum, turn north on U.S. 97, which winds through ranch country, then reenters the timber after a few miles in the Wenatchee Mountains, a spur of the Cascades. The old highway swings off the new one at a junction difficult to find—you'll just have to watch Forest Service signs for it—but the Blewett Pass highway is a good reminder of what highways were like

before apparently unlimited federal funds were available for roads. It twists and turns along the edge of a mountain and is so narrow in places that one has difficulty negotiating turns without backing up for another try. But the scenery is magnificent and the traffic very light.

Highway U.S. 97 joins U.S. 2 just a few miles west of **Wenatchee**, and the drive down the Wenatchee River through **Tumwater Canyon** to **Leavenworth** is one of the state's most beautiful drives. The Wenatchee shoots over a number of falls and rapids, cooling the air on those hot summer days and in October is one of the favorite drives for autumn color.

Completing the circle drive, you head west on U.S. 2, a two-lane highway that climbs to **Stevens Pass** through some of the prettiest Cascade scenery around: sheer mountainsides, tiny little meadows

Hikers in steadily increasing numbers battle their way up the mountain to the Enchantment Lakes for views such as this.

here and there, streams flowing past and beneath the highway, and no population to speak of.

From Stevens Pass U.S. 2 drops down into thick timber and follows the Skykomish River through the small towns of Skykomish, Baring, Gold Bar, Sultan, and Monroe. It passes beneath the stunning north face of Mt. Index, often highlighted by the evening sun flashing off its face.

By Rocky Mountain standards, these passes aren't especially terrorizing. Snoqualmie is only 3,010 feet; Swauk, 4,102; and Stevens, 4,061. But, as the contented say, they are sufficient.

Mountain Loop

It was the first autumn we were married, our first child was about six weeks old, and it was my first trip on the Mountain Loop Highway. My wife remembered it from her childhood and youth as one of the most pleasant day trips in the state, and I was anxious to see it. We owned a well-used car at the time, and since I was still a student, a tank of gas represented a major investment.

We drove to Snohomish, then north on Washington 9 and 92 toward **Granite Falls**. It was a beautiful fall day with the vine maple fiery red among the dark evergreen forest. We stopped for my first view of Granite Falls and the longest fish ladder in the world, then drove on to Verlot. We stopped at the small store and cafe for a milkshake

The Sauk River tumbles over boulders along the Mountain Loop Highway.

each, then proceeded on up the road that follows the bends in the Stillaguamish.

My wife was wearing white shorts and I was wearing old suntans. We weren't out of sight of Verlot when the car coughed inelegantly and died. It refused to start again. Being something of a mechanic in those days, I opened the hood and started a thorough investigation. About the time I found that the fuel pump had resigned from life, the seat of my suntans parted. I hid my underwear by wrapping a sweater around my waist. Then, less than five minutes later, the baby kicked and spilled the chocolate milkshake on my wife's white shorts. She covered that by hanging the baby's blanket down her front. Dressed in this fashion, we returned to the Verlot store and began making telephone calls.

Nobody was home. Nobody. Relatives, friends, casual acquaintances, all were somewhere else on that beautiful day. While my wife sat in one careful

47

position and I stood and walked with equal care, we pondered our situation. Finally, after more than an hour of fretting and calling, we located a friend at his parents' house. He went shopping for a new fuel pump and arrived with it at sundown. We had it on in a matter of minutes, and angry at the situation, we turned around and headed back to Seattle, leaving our friends far behind. I thought it strange that they didn't try to keep up with us. But I didn't slow up.

The next week we found why they were driving at such a sedate pace: They were poor students, too, and couldn't afford tires for their car. They had no spare and were driving on virtually threadbare tires, very carefully, very slowly. And if they had a flat on that trip, we would have left them stranded after they drove more than 75 miles to rescue us.

After that outing, we steered clear of the Mountain Loop Highway, and it was quite some time before I made the whole round trip. Too bad because it is one of the state's most beautiful drives. It runs along the South Fork of the Stillaguamish from Granite Falls through Robe, Verlot, Silverton to Barlow Pass with a side road to Monte Cristo. From there, it swings north to the logging town of Barrington, then returns west to Arlington.

It is an area rich in history, and an area that is going through a minor revival. Several books have been written recently about the area's history, and traces of the old railroad grade and bridges across the river still remain. **Silverton** was a major mining town at one time, and several of the homes and store buildings remain. At one time there was a famous hotel there, Big Four Inn, named for the mountain behind it. Unfortunately it was destroyed by fire several years ago.

All along the highway are turnouts for small campgrounds and picnic areas, also used by

The fish ladder at Granite Falls, covered by the steel grating, is reportedly the longest fish ladder in the world.

fishermen after salmon, steelhead, Dolly Varden, and rainbows. Hiking trails head off up into the mountains at odd intervals, and one of the most popular is **Bear Lake** near Verlot. Since we made our first camping trip there, the path has been paved to Bear Lake, and the trail to Pinnacle Lake high above it has been cleared and improved. Pinnacle is one of the prettiest lakes along the loop trip and is so high and protected from the sun by steep cliffs around it that it remains frozen far into the summer. Sharp needles of granite protrude from its center, giving it a rather sinister look, especially if you've packed a one-man raft up to it for fishing.

The old town of **Monte Cristo** is privately owned now, and a small admission is charged to enter and park there. Short hikes may be taken along a variety of trails leading out of the Swiss-style valley. You get an excellent view of the old town from the trail up toward Poodle Dog Pass. Food service, a gift shop, and a small museum occupy the former town site.

Numerous campsites are strung along the dirt road between Monte Cristo and Darrington, many secluded in heavy timber. Another sidetrip for the energetic is up a trail to **Goat Lake** about halfway between the two towns.

Darrington is a casual, unpretentious town noted for the number of loggers who live there, and the southern accents that reflect the loggers' origins. Old-time fiddling and other southern cultural activities are common there.

On the road between Darrington and Arlington are other good campsites and short hikes, particularly at **French Creek Campground**. It is primitive by most standards—no running water or electricity—but an excellent place to camp. A hike of less than a mile from the trailhead behind the campground takes you up the creek to a set of falls that drop hundreds of feet off a cliff. The trail continues on over the crest of the range, but most people stop at the falls or one of the shelters along the way for picnic lunches.

A suggestion: If you're camping at this or any other campground, avoid camping where the road curves. If you do, you'll get headlights from cars in your tent all night long.

North Cascades Highway

The North Cascades Highway isn't so new anymore—it was completed in 1972—but many people keep putting off a trip over it "until next year."

They shouldn't. It threads its way through some of the most beautiful stretches of scenery in the state. It doesn't carry the heavy traffic of I-90 across Snoqualmie, and the scenery is even more spectacular than is visible from U.S. 2 over Stevens Pass.

Until the highway was completed, the scenery was enjoyed only by hardy backpackers and pilots flying over the North Cascades National Park. But now everyone can enjoy the 125-mile route, an excellent weekend trip or one involving weeks while you sample all the trails and boat trips available on the route.

The North Cascades Highway (Washington 20) starts at Sedro Woolley and extends through the tiny town of Mazama in the eastern foothills of the Cascades to the famed Okanogan Country of north-central Washington. You will see one of the most modern two-lane highways built during the last decade between the upper end of Gorge Lake (about five miles east of Newhalem) to just west of Mazama. It has wide shoulders most of the way, and wider turnouts at viewpoints, some with parking spaces for 50 or more vehicles.

There are several campgrounds beginning on the west side at Colonial Creek on Ross Lake, part of Seattle City Light's popular Skagit River hydroelectric project. There are numerous trailheads along the highway, including an intersection with the **Pacific Crest Trail**, which starts several miles north at the Canadian border and ends at the Mexican border several hiking months away. It crosses at **Rainy Pass** at an elevation of 4,840 feet, where snow usually remains until after July 4 or all summer depending on the winter's supply and the summer's temperatures.

Rock climbers can be seen nearly every pretty day inching their way up the faces of mountains near the highway. You can always tell when they're out because travelers will be parked with binoculars to their eyes, watching them with the same fascination we watch high-wire acts.

The last call for fuel and food on your way east is Marblemount. The Forest Service station is a mile north of town, where you can pick up brochures and other information. The **North Cascades National Park Headquarters** at Sedro Woolley offers more information. You will need a wilderness permit if you're going backpacking in the park.

Next is **Newhalem**, a neat company town owned by Seattle City Light for employees of the dam project. An old steam engine beside the highway is a particular favorite for children, and City Light offers a six-hour tour of the dam and Diablo Lake, a ride on an incline railway, and a family-style meal. Advance reservations are required, however, and can be made in Seattle at City Light headquarters.

From Newhalem the highway clings to the rocky walls of Skagit Gorge, drills through the mountainside in tunnels, and crosses Gorge Lake. A mile-long side road takes you across **Diablo Dam** to a resort where boats, tackle, and motors are rented. You can hire transportation to the trailheads along the lake that lead up Big Beaver Valley and other attractions. The lake is particularly popular with canoeists and kayakers.

At Rainy Pass you can stroll along the Pacific Crest Trail (just to say you've been on it, if for no other reason) or hike over to Lake Ann, about 1½ miles away, where there is good trouting. You'll likely see marmots or hear them whistling to each other.

One of the most beautiful overlooks is at **Washington Pass**, at 5,477 feet the highest mountain pass in Washington on a highway. A side road leads to a rocky point where you can park and join the other shutter-bugs in what is perhaps the trip's scenic climax. The lofty, sharp pinnacles of Early Winters, Silver Star Mountain, Liberty Bell, and the Picket Range are spread out before you like a 3-D postcard.

Liberty Bell towers above the North Cascades Highway.

It is all downhill from here eastward to Mazama and Winthrop. Originally **Winthrop** was just another sleepy small town in a beautiful setting of mountains and clean, rushing streams. But with the coming of heavy seasonal traffic and the prospect of winter sports increasing, the town gave itself a massive facelift and now is a western town, complete with false-fronts, billboards painted on buildings, hitching posts, and whimsical artwork. A service station, for example, calls itself the "Fuel Yard."

Winthrop is in the **Methow Valley**, a pleasant, rural place with a distinct western atmosphere. It has dude ranches, horse ranches, and apple orchards. Small lakes are scattered in the foothills with boat and tackle rentals available for the excellent rainbow fishing.

The North Cascades Highway isn't always open year-round. If the winter snow is deep—as it usually is—and avalanche danger exists, the highway department closes it rather than spend large amounts of money keeping clear and risking avalanches that could take lives of motorists. Always check with the Washington State Patrol, highway department, or auto club in the winter and early spring before setting out on the trip.

Hiking

S pring is the time of year many of us get the urge to go back to nature, to strip ourselves of the last vestiges of civilization, and join the Neanderthal, the Natty Bumpos, and the foraging societies. We get a lump in our throats when we hear phrases such as "tuning in to nature," "accepting nature on her own terms," and "stripping our lives to essentials."

It is that last one that appeals to me, and I'm always grumbling about "things." Things and gadgets own us, I pontificate, and we shouldn't let that happen. Own only what you can carry on your back, I say.

So what do I carry on my back when I hike back to nature? A backpack made of aircraft aluminum alloy, coated nylon sack, and a padded hipbelt filled with a petrochemical foam. Nylon-coated raingear. Silicone waterproofing for my vegetable-oil tanned boots. Aluminum pots and pans. A stainless steel cup. Polarized sunglasses. Reprocessed wool-and-nylon shirt. Freeze-dried and dehydrated food in plastic containers. Nylon-taffeta tent with coated nylon rain fly, nylon guy lines, aluminum stakes, and fiberglass poles.

Add to this the cameras and lenses, sophisticated brass stove, white gas, plastic bottles, crystals for soft drinks, and a dozen or so other "necessities" that would have made

A young hiker emerges from her tent to begin a day in Esmerelda Basin.

The family paused for a snack and hot chocolate while waiting to see how long a Memorial Day snowstorm would last.

Meriwether Lewis blink and scratch his fleas—I'll bet he would have loved a bottle of *Off*.

Such thoughts cross our minds when we begin the year's hiking season and our backpacking muscles aren't toughened up. There are few hikers who, on such first days, don't wonder why they didn't fire up the barbecue in the backyard instead of subjecting themselves to the discomforts of the trail. Any backpacker will tell you there is no such thing as a comfortable pack or a pair of boots that don't hurt sometime during the season.

But it is the countryside that makes the trip seem necessary and the discomforts worthwhile. Washington offers some of the most exciting backpacking in the nation, everything from high alpine scenery to dense, low-level forests to the open, high arid lands of the eastern Cascades or wild ocean beaches.

Some of our most pleasant memories of family outings come from hikes we've taken in Washington. One summer, for example, we decided to concentrate on **Mt. Rainier National Park**, in spite of the crowds there and our determination to find places that everyone else didn't know about. Perhaps such places exist, but it is doubtful they are all that beautiful or someone, surely, would have already discovered them and told a friend who told some friends who told . . . .

Our first hike in the Mt. Rainier shadow wasn't exactly thrilling. We arrived late, and most campsites were already taken along the trails, so the rangers sent us on one that wasn't heavily used. It was between seven and eight miles long, had several streams along the way and campsites at the end near the snow. But he neglected to tell us that all along the hike we could hear highway traffic less than half a mile away, which doesn't contribute to a wilderness experience. And when we reached the campground at the end, we pulled out our new dome tent with its aluminum poles we so painstakingly lashed together with shock cords and found one of the poles broken. So we stayed in a fancy tent with a suspicious point on one side and hoped nobody would notice. Of course they did, and we had to explain the wound in the tent several times and listen to the advice so generously given by dedicated backpackers.

There have been many, many other hikes of various lengths, from day hikes to week-long hikes that give children a fund of memories to draw on in their later years.

The popularity of hiking is proven by the vast library of guidebooks to the sport. It is almost unbelievable the number of such guides that have been published and are coming out at a steady pace each year. They represent a virtual industry in themselves, and more than one writer has wished for a monopoly on them.

Obviously not all hikes require the strength of a backpacker or the wisdom of a mountain man (although basic common sense doesn't hurt). Some can be made in a day or less by anyone who can walk, and not all these are in one of the larger city parks. An example is the hike from **Lake Ozette** out to **Cape Alava**, where an important archaeological dig is in progress, down the beach to Sand Point, and back to Lake Ozette. Each of the three legs of this triangular hike are three miles long, and all of the trail from Ozette to the beach at Cape Alava is on a boardwalk.

There is hardly a summer without a tragedy in the mountains, and almost always it involves someone unprepared for changes in weather. The technical term now is hypothermia, but it used to be called "exposure." So go prepared for the worst kind of weather and be pleasantly surprised if the weather remains warm and fair. Consider the extra gear you carry an insurance policy.

I suppose the favorite hike our family has gone on was one where little or nothing of great adventure happened. We joined friends and drove over to **Esmerelda Basin,** out of Cle Elum, one Memorial Day weekend. Since there weren't too many hikers around, we found a campsite close to a seasonal stream in the heart of the basin and camped there the first night. Since nobody came by bothering us that afternoon or evening, or even the following morning, we decided to risk theft (remember, this was years ago) and use the basin as a base camp for day hikes. Our children were all young, and we couldn't take long treks.

The next day we decided to go over one of the passes and down to Stuart Lake, a hike of about seven miles round trip. We packed lunches, snacks, foul-weather gear, and other necessities in three adult packs and started the climb up to Long's

Pass in bright sunshine. We took our time, stopping often to gaze Ferdinand-like at the new flowers coming up just behind the receding snow, and reached a level spot immediately below the summit of the pass shortly after noon.

We decided to pause there for lunch and to see what the weather was going to do, since it had become cloudy. While we ate, we watched clouds fill a gap in the mountains far to the west, then move swiftly toward us. When the low cloud arrived, we found ourselves in a snowstorm that gave us a few anxious moments. While we were equipped for such an emergency, it wasn't part of our weekend plans. We put more water on the stoves to heat for tea, coffee, and hot chocolate, hunched down in a temporary shelter in the lee of some boulders, and waited.

The snowstorm soon passed, but it left behind a particularly nasty, wet and cold wind that cut through our clothing. We couldn't tell what the weather was like back at our base camp, but we decided we'd better go back that way rather than going on over the nearby pass and trying to make Stuart Lake that day. Back at camp the sun was shining, and the cold wind on the mountain had become a refreshing breeze below.

The next day we hiked up toward another pass at the far end of the basin, marveling at the sheer mountain faces from which snow and ice still clung. Although we were soon walking in snow, beating trails for the children so they wouldn't disappear into drifts, the weather was very pleasant, warm with an occasional breeze.

We stopped for lunch at the ruins of a miner's cabin, and were thinking of walking over to the walls of the mountains that rose straight up from the valley floor. But before we walked over, we heard something that sounded like a sonic boom and assumed that was what we heard. But then one of the children pointed above and shouted, "Look at that! Wow!"

High up on the walls vast chunks of solid ice were falling off and dropping to the valley floor near us with a resounding boom, followed by a shattering and tumbling sound. So much for walking over to the wall.

True, almost nothing happened that weekend. We didn't hike far and we barely cleared timberline. But we remember that hike with particular warmth. Today we wouldn't dare take our children on such a tame outing because they would want to hike as far and as hard as they could, then climb a nearby peak for good measure. Or, they would insist they bring a gang of friends to keep it interesting. However, they often speak of that weekend with the same attitude. By expedition hikers' standards, it wasn't much. By our standards, it was sufficient.

Now that our children are old enough to go on their own outings in the mountains and manage to make three or four hikes with school groups during the school year, we are losing interest in self-imposed discomfort. However, there are some dream hikes we would like to make before the knees and lungs completely rebel.

One such hike is a portion, if not all, of the Pacific Crest Trail that runs the length of the state, from the Canadian border to the Columbia River. The Washington trail is just over 450 miles, but it can be divided into individual hikes, such as between Rainy Pass on the North Cascades Highway to Stevens Pass.

Western pasqueflower.

Another dream hike is into the Enchantment Lakes out of Leavenworth during the winter. This could be a punishing trip, one that could result in a long stay if caught by a storm. But a party properly prepared and in good physical condition could have an enviable experience.

Still another is hiking the entire length of the Olympic National Park's coastal strip. Walking on loose sand and scrambling over headlands in heavy rain may not sound like outright fun, but somehow such outings are rewarding. They show how much or how little one can do.

Chelan

For decades one of the most popular outings in Central Washington has been the boat ride from the town of Chelan up the lake by the same name to the very end 55 miles away at the town of Stehekin, which is isolated from lack of roads. The boat leaves the dock at about 8:30 a.m. and arrives at noon, then leaves again half an hour later for the return.

Lake Chelan is a relic of the Ice Age in a valley scooped out by glaciers. It is long and narrow as it follows the valley it flooded, seldom more than two miles wide. It is a deep lake—nearly 1,500 feet at the deepest place measured.

Stehekin has become something of a recreational boomtown with the North Cascades National Park in existence, and virtually the entire town has been turned into a concession.

Some hikers come into the town from the west side of the Cascades at Cascade Pass. Many other trails lead away from the lake.

The Man Who Was Afraid of Bears

We devoted one summer to Mt. Rainier (see Hiking) and never really did cover all approaches to the massive volcano thoroughly. But, the hikes were for the most part worth the effort, and like the Pacific Crest Trail and a trip down the Mackenzie River, we will probably never get around to making the complete Wonderland Trail hike around Mt. Rainier.

One of our hikes took us up to Indian Henry's Hunting Ground with overnight camping permitted only part way near Devils Canyon. We got a late start and didn't arrive at the campsite until nearly dark. Two daughters were ahead of the pack, and just as they walked past a small tent near the trail, out jumped a stocky middle-aged man and almost shouted, "Howdy!" The girls nearly took to their heels but waited for reinforcements to arrive.

The man introduced himself as an airline employee from a southern state, traveling alone for a weekend and fulfilling a long-time dream: visiting Mt. Rainier National Park. The trouble was that he didn't know the country, had a heart condition, and was afraid to travel alone. He attached himself to our small group throughout the evening and tried to interest our son with his Boy Scout stories, which tended to sound more like Sunday School picnics than wilderness trips. But, he was pleasant and we didn't mind his company.

The next morning he was perched on a log outside our tents before we got up, then retreated to his tent while we had breakfast. We told him we were hiking on up to Indian Henry's later in the morning and taking a lunch and that he was invited if he cared to join us. He declined and said he would hang around camp that day, and if we wanted to leave our tents and gear there, he would be happy to watch over them. We were going to leave the gear anyway, but thanked him for the offer. We headed on up the trail to the beautiful meadow with the mountain hanging behind like a wall mural.

As we walked past his tent, he had a forlorn and rather frightened look on his face, and he called me aside. "Say, can you tell me if there are any bears up here?" he asked.

Not knowing if he wanted to see them desperately or if he was desperately afraid of them, I told him that there were black bears all over the Cascades, "but, of course, they're harmless."

He looked at me, apparently uncertain if I was honest or if my judgment could be trusted.

"What time do you think you'll be back?" he asked. I told him in about three hours, more or less. In time for dinner at any rate. He nodded and we went on.

We weren't more than half a mile down the trail before we saw him coming along behind. We stopped to wait, and after he caught up with us and took a breather on a log, he told us to just go on ahead; he'd wander around and look at flowers and that kind of thing. Just out for a little leg stretcher.

We went on to Indian Henry's and had our lunch at a picnic table near the cabin, and waded around in the snow that still was about two feet deep in the meadow.

Soon he appeared. He looked a bit gray and ashen from the climb and appeared glad to see us. At last convinced that he wanted to be with us constantly, we told him to just travel with us on the way back, and we'd have dinner together. He declined—said he would poke around there awhile, maybe walk down the trail and see what was on the other side of the meadow, and he'd see us that night.

But he kept us in sight all the way back to our tents and joined us for dinner that night, asking again and again about bears. We resisted the natural impulse to tell bear stories from Yukon, knowing they would terrify him and make sleep impossible for him that night. We continued soothing him on the subject.

He hiked with us the next day as we returned to Longmire, and we decided to camp in the campground that evening among the RVs. The campground was about two miles from Longmire, and there were six of us in a small Maverick. We dropped off everyone and everything at a campsite, then went back for him. He had that forlorn look until he recognized us and hustled into the car with his pack. He pitched his tent near ours, went to the slide show with us, and turned in at about the same time.

The next morning as we prepared to leave, he

pondered how he would return to Sea-Tac airport that day. We made several suggestions, such as asking around the campground and checking with a ranger, but he tended to cling to our family group even though it was obvious that he couldn't ride with us unless we abandoned a child. We offered him a ride back down to Longmire, but he declined, saying he would stay at the campground.

He had his tent put away and his pack ready to go long before we did, and he sat and watched us break camp. When everything was in and on the car, he walked over to, we assumed, tell us goodbye.

"Say, old buddy," he said. "Were you telling me the truth about bears?"

I assured him I was and resisted the temptation to tell him to ask a ranger if he didn't believe me. He just looked at me, as if I were taking him snipe hunting, nodded, and stepped away from the car.

Did we ruin his stories he planned to tell when he went back home? What on earth was a frightened man with a heart condition doing on the edge of Mt. Rainier by himself anyway?

We exchanged addresses, and when we got home, I sent him a book I'd promised him. That was in 1974 and we still haven't heard from him.

A day hiker stops for a sip of cold water from a stream in Mt. Rainier National Park.

59

Skiing

Skiing is probably the most popular sport among our children. While some of them lean toward various indoor sports, such as basketball and volleyball, skiing definitely takes first place in outdoor sports for them. By now they have skied at nearly all the slopes in the Cascades, and we have future winter trips planned to those in north-central Washington, in the Spokane area, and down in the Blue Mountains. All are veterans of a ski school, including the business of our getting up on Saturday mornings at an hour sometimes reserved for people going *to* bed.

Skiing is a cultural function in Washington. If steelheading and salmon fishing are part of the Washington mystique, then skiing is part of its culture. And no wonder, because skiing is so convenient to the large population centers. All the way from the Canadian border down to Oregon, ski slopes are hardly more than a hour's drive from any city. You can leave a rainy morning at sea level and an hour later be in near-zero weather with snow 14 feet deep and still falling.

During the past few years other forms of snow recreation have become more and more popular, particularly cross-country skiing and to a lesser extent, snowshoeing. These pursuits are in part a reaction to the crowded ski slopes and the expense involved in outfitting with "proper" downhill equipment. While downhill equipment costs as much as sin, cross-country and snowshoeing equipment is relatively inexpensive. And there is also the matter of solitude, so important to many while pursuing their recreation. While downhill slopes are jammed with people, and lines at the lifts sometimes involve waits up to half an hour, none of this applies to cross-country skiing and snowshoeing. An old logging road, an open meadow, a trail, or high alpine country all make excellent places for these more solitary sports.

However, before trying them be certain you understand the dangers inherent to any sport in cold weather—hypothermia, getting lost, snow blindness, avalanches, and possible injuries. Few get themselves into trouble on these kinds of outings, but winter is an unforgiving season. For this reason, it is best to travel in groups with several members of the group experienced in the sport. While it may not lead to total solitude, it will lead to safety.

Another solution is to try these sports with experienced guides and outfitters. There are several in Washington, particularly Northwest Alpine Guide Service of Seattle, which operates year-round to include backpacking, climbing, whitewater, and other wilderness sports. Another is Family Adventures of Leavenworth. This

A ski casualty is turned into a work of art by older brothers and sisters.

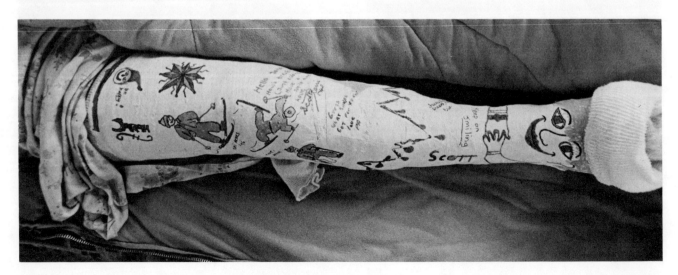

60

organization has back-country camps with wall tents out in the wilderness where the only motorized vehicle you'll hear is the sno-cat that takes you out and back.

We've never gone on one of the Family Adventures expeditions, but we did spend a night in one of their wall tents and can vouch for their warmth. We were there in May, an awkward time because there wasn't enough snow for skiing or snowshoeing, but too much for hiking. It was still cold, and we snuggled into the sleeping bags that night waiting impatiently for our body to warm the bags. But the next morning was a different matter. All I had to do was stick one arm out into the cold and light the fire in the little woodstove in the tent. Within five minutes the tent was as warm as a farm kitchen on Christmas morning—a highlight of the weekend.

While the children have always done most of their skiing by taking buses to the slopes either with a ski school or through a school program, nearly every winter we have arranged to spend a long weekend or Christmas vacation week at the slopes as a family. We've usually rented a motorhome because it enables us to spend the night in the parking lot and save the drive,

frequently harrowing, up the icy road every morning to the slopes. Motorhomes are a good way to spend such weekends because one year we had to visit three slopes before finding enough snow for good skiing.

But motorhomes have their limitations, like everything else. They get smaller and smaller as our family grows and more and more difficult to keep clean and dry as people track in snow and dirt. And, they are heir to all the problems of a home and an automobile combined. If you're not having trouble with the automotive equipment, you're having trouble with the home equipment. You're constantly battling frozen water pipes on models not designed for cold weather (check out this aspect before renting), the furnace doesn't work, or no matter how wide the vents are opened, you have condensation dripping on you all night. Yet we enjoy them for the freedom of movement they offer.

The other alternative is renting a condominium, motel room, or chalet for such an occasion. The problems with these range from being too expensive, being too close to people who party loudly every night, or having to drive back and forth to the slopes every day. There are disadvantages no matter which method you choose. And, since I have decided that skiing is a sport I must live without or I'll never get a word written, my opinions may be a bit slanted toward those who choose to stay inside while the others play.

61

A ski racer ends a run rather ignominiously while others look the other way.

George and His Friends

We still wonder what happened to George and his friends.

Northwest Alpine Guide Service made us an offer one winter that proved irresistible. They asked us along as guests on a cross-country skiing trip to Lake Wenatchee. They hoped I would write a story about it for the *Seattle Post-Intelligencer*, which I did. They were confident enough of their operation to just turn us loose among the rest of their guests without the preferential treatment some newspaper people expect. If any of their clients knew we got a better price than the rest, we saw no indication.

At that time the guide service had an arrangement with an inn at the head of Lake Wenatchee. Guests stayed there, ate all their meals in the inn, and took lunches provided by the inn on the day-long trips.

The inn was rundown at that time. Most of the rooms upstairs had no doors on them, and curtains gave some privacy but no security. The doors to a few rooms wouldn't close properly and certainly wouldn't lock. But the owners were casual and friendly, the homemade bread delicious, and the meals superb. Some musicians living in the area, none less than 70 years old, appeared at night to sing and play hillbilly and old-time fiddlin' music. When they left, we listened to classics and jazz on the stereo system.

The next morning we met George. We were supposed to be up at 6:30. They said only that they'd get us up, since obviously there were no telephones in the room.

Lunch time in shirt-sleeve weather for cross-country skiers above Lake Wenatchee.

62

George got us up. George was a huge mutt that looked like he was part Labrador and part shepherd. George had hung around the inn politely the previous evening, bothering no one. But in the morning he became a servant. Since the doors couldn't keep anything else out, they permitted George immediate access to the sleepers. He went into each room and nudged people awake, then stood aside to be sure they were indeed getting out of bed. If they didn't, George would gently, firmly grasp a blanket or a pajama sleeve and begin tugging. He left you no choice but get up and get dressed.

All up and down the hall we heard people saying, "Okay, George. I'm up George. Go get somebody else up, George."

It made for a lot of conversation at breakfast and loosened up the strangers considerably.

Other than a respect for George's manners, my other memory of that weekend was my discovery of how much I hated cross-country skiing. I'd never done it before and was no more graceful than a drunken ape on roller skates. All day long I felt as if those skinny boards were clipped to my toenails. I decided then that if I wanted to see anything in that area, I could wait until the snow melted and I could walk out in the meadows and up the hills. Never have I become acquainted with a sport I disliked more intensely and more immediately than cross-country skiing.

So George, that gentle soul, balanced out my weekend. His owners left the inn shortly afterward. If they are in the business of dealing with overnight guests, I hope they've kept George. Like the perfect maid in a Somerset Maugham story, George couldn't be replaced by a telephone, a bell, a man, woman, or child.

Cross-country skiing avoids the crowded slopes of the downhillers—can open up backcountry on a sunny day.

Cheap Snow Play

For awhile we felt something like reverse snobs whenever we joined our skiing children for a chilly day on the slopes. While they paraded in their brightly colored clothing and name-brand skis, we took our inflated innertubes to a snow-play area and bumped and rolled down the slope.

As these photos show, inner-tubing may not have the finesse of skis, but it looks like a lot more fun to a non-skier.

Steelheading

Not long after we were married, my wife's brother-in-law decided it was time to educate me in the ways of this corner of the land. He outfitted me with a pair of hip boots and a rubber-bootie insert that was supposed to keep my feet warm (and didn't). He loaned me one of his two hand warmers, fixed up a spare rod and reel and some lures, and told me to dress warmly. He picked me up one cold morning before dawn—long before dawn—and we drove north of Seattle to Arlington, crossed a bridge somewhere on the Stillaguamish River, turned down a dirt road, and parked. We walked down a cow path past some farm buildings and joined a group of men strung out along the river.

We were going steelheading.

He coached me on the ways of casting, drifting, then casting, and drifting all over again. Then we waded into the river. The water at this time of year was chilly—so chilly that chunks of ice kept hitting me in the backs of my legs, and the line and guides on my rod froze solid. He instructed me to dip the pole into the river to clear the ice, which I did. I also shifted the hand warmer from pocket to pocket but kept it in my right pocket most of the time, because I could not cast and thumb the reel to prevent backlashes with gloves on.

All around us were less hardy men who built fires on the gravel bank and simply let their lures lie on the bottom waiting for fish. My partner in the enterprise was too much a purist for that, and I went along because I was too conscious of the hardy outdoorsman image I was trying to create for the family into which I had so recently married. So, I stood there in the freezing water, my feet aching, my hands numb, my nose running, and my eyes watering, trying to catch a fish that I probably wouldn't even want to eat.

This went on until shortly after noon, and he had caught one nice steelhead. Maybe I had some strikes, and maybe I didn't. I couldn't tell the difference between a steelhead strike and the lure catching on a rock. My brother-in-law wasn't much help either. He said there was no way to describe a steelhead strike, except that after you caught your first one, you'd know the difference between a strike and a rock. Probably not before.

It took me years in Washington to admit how idiotic I was that day. I don't mind a bit of discomfort and, like many outdoors people, have looked forward with great anticipation to trips that would involve a degree of pain and discomfort, if not danger. But not to catch a fish. While I haven't been steelheading since, it has taken me all these years to admit freely to one and all that, to me, steelheading is a stupid way to spend a day, just as a lot of steelheaders cannot understand why anyone would go nearly 2,000 miles to float down a river without wetting a line.

There has been a mythology erected around steelheading, and it is impossible to understand the attraction of this part of the country without having a nodding acquaintance with steelheading, rock climbing, kayaking, and clam digging—to name a few. Or, as someone once pointed out to me, if people will sit in a football stadium when the temperature is 40 degrees below freezing, what's so strange about steelheading? At least it puts meat on the table, even if it does freeze some meat on the fisherman in the process.

67

The photographer, Jan Fardell, labeled this "Three Quacks East and One Quack West."

Ice Fishing

A few days before this was written, one of our children returned from a snowshoeing trip and said the group had pitched their tents on a small lake that was covered with snow.

"The next morning we chopped holes in the ice for water and guess what—the lake wasn't frozen solid. It was just slush. But it wasn't very deep, only about four feet where we camped."

Four feet! we screamed. Four feet of water with a tent wrapped around you might as well be 40 feet. Parents get spooked easily, especially when we remember waltzing across frozen ponds and lakes as a child and watching with more fascination than fear as the ice bent and rippled, creaking, groaning, or actually cracking beneath our feet.

But, judging from comments by the people I've talked to about ice fishing, the ice itself is the least of their worries. The technique of catching fish is what occupies their minds, and they assume anyone trying this stoical sport will have sense enough to fish only on ice thick enough to support an AMTRAK train.

Ice Skaters take advantage of six-inch-thick ice on Alkali Lake in the Columbia Basin. Lakes throughout this area are favorites of ice fishermen.

68

Snow lingers late—sometimes throughout the summer—in the higher reaches of the Cascades and Olympics.

Having never tried the sport, I'll yield to the experts in the field, Blaine Freer of the *Seattle P-I* and Fred Peterson, who know their fishing.

They say the best rig is a nine-foot flyrod with a sensitive tip, unless you use a bobber, which means you can use anything you want. They say fish tend to nibble more in the winter, and this makes a good bobber important. The best bobbers are made of quills, not plastic, because quills are more sensitive to the slightest nibble.

They recommend borrowing your child's sled to haul your gear out onto the ice. It will also keep gear off the ice and dry when the sun begins thawing ice or snow. The sled is where you should have your fire in a can or your portable heater or campstove. If you build a fire on the ice, you're liable to see it melt its own hole and disappear forever.

Insulated boots are so strongly recommended you should consider them a requirement. Also, wear insulated underwear and plenty of overwear.

The hole? Some use a hatchet or an axe to chop it. Others use a chainsaw and still others use a long auger. The last two mentioned are the best, and almost anything is better than the chisels some use. Remember how sensitive your hands are when they're cold, and what smarts more than a cold mashed thumb?

Back to the heating process—some fishermen lug out a five-gallon can filled with *Presto* logs, and others take a like amount of charcoal briquettes. Some take along portable gasoline or kerosene heaters, and a few even build tentlike windbreaks over the holes to trap more heat and keep the wind off.

For bait, my experts recommend worms, salmon eggs, or cooked corn. Don't use sinkers; instead, let the bait drift around on its own. If you don't get a bite in half an hour, chop another hole. Keep moving around until you start hauling in the fish.

The best ice-fishing lakes, they say, are in the Columbia Basin Project and along the eastern slopes of the Cascade Range. Another good one is Whitestone Lake in Okanogan County. Some of the best are Roses, Mud, Alkali, Crescent Bay, Banks, Hog Canyon (Spokane County), Cle Elum, Kachess, and the Potholes.

Now. Go forth and freeze.

Horse Packer

One of our children talks to horses and insists the horses talk back. We tend to believe her because she controls horses like nobody else in the family. Even after growing up on a farm with workhorses and spending some time on cattle ranches as a youth, I still feel like an imposter while aboard a horse. And the horse invariably knows it.

However, since we became acquainted with Norm Trapp and his family and stop by to visit them occasionally at their small ranch near Merritt just east of Stevens Pass, we felt we owed it to ourselves to take a trip with the Trapps. We did so the summer we decided to spend our entire vacation within Washington. But only a day trip scheduled between Norm's other trips.

Like many horse packers in the state, Norm performs a variety of chores. He sometimes meets groups of hikers on long trips with the next week's supply of food. Sometimes a government agency will contract with him to take surveyors or study teams back into the wilderness for several days at a time. He takes big-game hunters out in the fall. And occasionally he will get drop-in business from his location on the highway.

We were in the last category. We had cut short a trip to another part of the state because the promises printed in brochures and repeated in a telephone conversation were not kept. Unwilling to return home to the lawn that needed mowing, we stopped and asked Norm if he was available for a day trip. He was, two days later, so we camped at a Department of Natural Resources primitive campground nearby and lazed around until the trip.

The horses were gentle, but padded saddles are frowned upon no matter how sore one becomes after a day of riding.

We hadn't specified where we wanted to go, so Norm decided a trip up Nason Ridge behind his ranch would be a good one. We met him at a trailhead, saddled up, and started up the steep trail. We fought the brush until we emerged from the timber into an open meadow. From there on we were only occasionally in sparse timber that grows in little draws or other protected areas.

By this time, of course, all of us were feeling the saddle, and when we stopped for a rest, we were already stiff and sore. Except for the girl who talks to horses. From the meadow we could see Mt. Rainier far off to the south, and we would see all the other Cascade mountains later on the trail.

We mounted the horses again and followed the crest of the ridge to the west toward a Forest Service lookout. At one point I looked back just in time to see our six-year-old topple off her pony flat onto the ground. We went back and found that she had fallen asleep, and only her pride suffered. She got back on and took a firm grip on the saddle horn, telling the rest of us to leave her alone. We did, and that was her last nap until we drove home.

We had our lunch at the lookout tower manned (if you'll pardon the expression) by a college girl from the Wenatchee area. No, she didn't get lonely. She liked to read, liked to be alone, and enjoyed the beauty of the mountains. True, it got a little scary

While the riders took a badly needed break, the horses grazed in a high meadow with a view.

when thunderstorms hit, but that was part of the excitement. And no, she hadn't reported any fires.

While talking to her, I remembered one of my disastrous Boy Scout projects as a boy back in Missouri. I was going to get a merit badge for building a lookout tower. Usually the towers were two- or three-boy projects, but I had no Boy Scout friends near our farm, and I wanted to build it myself. So, my head filled with fantasies of standing in my lookout tower and saving the entire county because I spotted a fire, I built it. But I built it out of skinny, bendably saplings. It literally never got off the ground. When we sold the farm and moved away, the poles were still lying in an untidy pile on that knoll.

This lookout bore absolutely no resemblance to mine. It was cozy with a stove that was used for both cooking and heat. The young woman had a two-way radio plus her own transistor radio, stacks of books, cupboards filled with food, water, and wood brought in by either pack train or helicopter—plus a 360-degree view of the Cascade Range.

I thought the ride back would never end. Going uphill on a horse isn't bad at all. Going downhill on a horse, mile after mile, is agony. I got off and walked, but the horse kept nudging me ahead with his head or stepping on my heels. So I rode, my legs raw on the outside were feeling bent inside. The rest of the family either didn't hurt as much as I did or were more stoical. Probably the latter.

I haven't been on a horse since.

Puget Sound is another of those Washington features that defies exact description. More than Seattle, the Sound has represented home to me for the past two decades. Strangely, we don't live in a home with a view of it. We don't own a boat, and we seldom go out on it in a boat. When we lived in Longview I was offered a job in Portland, a good place to live and work. But we wanted to come home. The Sound represented home, and Seattle seemed the most reasonable place to live near it.

After all this time, we still know very little about all the islands in the Sound, and when people begin talking about their sailing trips, I suspect my eyes glaze over because sailing, unless it is ocean sailing, interests me not at all. Unless we were planning a trip up the Inside Passage, or down the West Coast and across to the Pacific Islands, sailing seems an awfully expensive way to play.

Part of the Sound's charm or attraction to me is that, like other people, I get some comfort in living on a boundary—the frontier between land and sea. Maybe it is an attraction stored in our genes from the time when life first left the sea never to return.

A Sunday Afternoon

It was an autumn day, warm with a slight breeze that blew in those heavy mists—wet as rain but softer on the face—that muted rather than obscured the shoreline of Puget Sound. The sun appeared briefly in random spots, emphasizing rather than illuminating the water and the gray-green land surrounding it.

We were alone on the open deck of the ferry as we crossed to Southworth. Traffic was light as we drove north. When we turned off the main highway back toward the Sound, we were alone on a road so narrow that the fern and berry vines scraped the side of the car. Rain-laden evergreen branches drooped toward the road, sheltering it so much that my friend turned on the headlights.

We parked in a driveway, so narrow and crowded by ferns that we were soaked to our knees before we got to the door of the small house. The house was invisible from the road and blocked from neighbors' view by natural growth. It sat high on a

bluff overlooking the Sound with a small border of lawn separating it from more underbrush before the bluff dropped off abruptly into the water. Neat and unpretentious, the unstained cedar-shake house had only one splash of color showing from the driveway—a group of brightly colored bottles in the kitchen window.

We were met at the door by an elderly woman, slender, straight, and lively. She held out both hands to my companion, touched her cheek to his chest briefly, then turned to acknowledge my presence. She accepted the large can of mixed nuts he brought her with a gentle joke about his catering to her vices, then explained to me that she was addicted to nuts and always dug around like a frantic squirrel for the brazil nuts first.

Like the woman, the kitchen through which we entered was unpretentious, neat, and with few frills. The only odor I detected was that of cheese and crackers in a serving dish, and a metal pot of coffee bubbling quietly on the stove. The living room stretched the length of the small house with large windows on either side of the door. The furniture was spartan—wooden frames with foam-rubber cushions and two wicker chairs with bright cushions. There were few knick-knacks, but two superb watercolors of tugboats hung on the wall. The dominant feature was a beautifully polished piano with slightly yellowed keys, worn in spots like the stone steps to a library. Chopin, Mozart and Rachmaninoff were represented on the music rack.

While she worked in the kitchen, she cheerfully chided us for being single at such a late stage of life and told me of her unsuccessful matchmaking attempts on my friend. Then she came out with the tray laden with cheese, crackers, nuts, and coffee and kept the comfortable conversation going, she and my friend bringing each other up to date on their lives and establishing me as a student working part-time with my friend.

Then, in a low voice, my friend asked about her husband. She said he would be coming out soon, then told me that her husband was suffering from a terminal illness and was confined to bed except for brief periods in the wheel chair. The doctor had recommended that he be hospitalized until "the end" came, but she wouldn't permit it.

They had been married more than 40 years and had never been apart more than two or three days during that time. They were childless and they considered each other their best friends, "and one does not send one's best friend away to die among strangers." So she learned how to care for him and kept him home. She warned us he was sensitive of his appearance, and when he came out to please not offer to shake hands because they were swollen and he kept them hidden. He would stay only a few minutes, then return to bed.

After a few minutes, she excused herself and went into the bedroom. We heard low voices and shared laughter before they came into the living room, he in the wheelchair and she behind. He kept his entire body beneath his neck covered with a bright blanket and spoke briefly to us, asking my friend about mutual acquaintances and his job. Less than 10 minutes elapsed before he thanked us for coming and returned to the bedroom.

When she came out again, she said he sat in front of the window two or three times a day looking out across the water on which he had sailed for both pleasure and for a livelihood on tug boats. She said he loved Puget Sound more than anyone she knew, and that he had often said he'd rather watch it than a film because it, too, constantly changed.

My friend asked her to play the piano, but she declined firmly and with obvious regret. She hadn't been practicing lately and arthritis was stiffening her fingers. She went to a small room off the kitchen and returned with a large portable radio and found a station playing classical music. Bach was good Sunday afternoon music, she said, and she knew from a schedule printed in a newspaper that some of his organ and cello music was being played that afternoon. She turned it on with a volume level that permitted us to either listen or talk. We did both, and there were those long periods of silence that comes from comfort among people rather than boredom or discomfort.

I don't remember what we talked about the remainder of the afternoon, but I do remember being completely at ease while, for the first time since moving to Washington, seeing what I have come to consider the true beauty of Puget Sound. While we sat facing the window and listening to the orderly, dignified music of Bach, I watched the subtle changes on the water. The rain never completely ceased nor did it ever fall in large drops. The sky and water went through virtually every shade of blue and gray as low clouds swept across the Sound from west to east. Although the house faced Seattle, we seldom saw its skyline. Instead, only a lighter colored stretch of shoreline appeared occasionally through the mist.

Toward the close of the day, the sun finally broke through a small opening in the clouds and cast a streamer of light in a long, slanting angle that ended on a tiny point of land within a quarter of a mile of the house. It stayed there for perhaps a

A hungry gull performs a minuet-like maneuver.

minute, no longer, then the clouds closed, and the sun didn't appear again that day. The day seemed much darker than before, and the far shoreline disappeared.

There was a primeval quality to the day, and from our vantage point only three basic elements were shown—land, water, and rain. I remember commenting to our hostess that it was as if the processes of creation were still at work and that no man had ever been here yet.

She agreed and said it was one of the attractions of Puget Sound to her and her husband. On days such as this one, she said, they were unaware of other people and the things those people were doing to the water and shoreline because they could not be seen. It gave her the feeling that Puget Sound was timeless; on such

days the region must look exactly as it did when the last glaciers departed. Somehow, the thought comforted her, she said.

That afternoon was in late autumn. A few weeks later my friend told me that her husband had died and that the woman would continue living in the house. I never saw her again. I've forgotten her name by now, and it has been more than a decade since I saw the friend with whom I visited her.

But that afternoon is my lasting impression of Puget Sound; an elderly couple living in quiet dignity, deeply in love all their married years, living where they wanted to, and enjoying it quietly as people do with very personal things.

But most of all I remember sitting for an entire afternoon looking at Puget Sound, for the first time really studying it and its timeless elemental beauty. Bach will forever be implanted in my mind as the proper music for Sunday afternoons with a view of Puget Sound.

A fishing boat heads back to the dock toward the end of the day.

77

Ferries

It happens almost every April Fool's Day. The ferries that run back and forth across Puget Sound are double-ended with controls, propellers, and ramps at each end so they don't have to be turned around every time they dock. The result is that regular passengers know exactly where everything is, and those who commute to work form specific habits. They have favorite seats and head for them as automatically and unthinkingly as commuters across the Evergreen Point Floating Bridge drop their toll in outstretched hands.

However, on April Fool's Day, skippers with a sense of humor *do* turn the ferries around, and the crews delight in watching the passengers head for their favorite spots—which aren't there. They're on the other side. There are always a lot of milling around, quizzical looks, and good-natured laughter as they discover they've been suckered again.

The Washington State Ferries are as much a part of Puget Sound life as foggy mornings. Out-of-state guests often express amazement that we can take something so romantic as a salt-water ferry for granted. After all, you can even charter them for private parties. And you can pack a picnic lunch and ride one for more than two hours through some of the most beautiful scenery on Puget Sound for little more than a buck, if you walk aboard.

Residents of Bainbridge and Vashon Islands live lives regulated to a great extent by ferry schedules, and hostesses in Seattle are not disturbed in the least when a couple leaves before dessert because they have to catch a ferry. It is part of the way of life here.

Most of the ferries are used simply to reduce the mileage between the Kitsap and Olympic Peninsulas. Those connecting with Seattle cross the Sound to Vashon and Bainbridge Islands and to Bremerton. Another route connects Edmonds on the mainland with Kingston on the Kitsap Peninsula. Another runs from Mukilteo to Columbia Beach on Whidbey Island. Shorter runs are between Point Defiance in Tacoma and Tahlequah on Vashon Island, and between Port Townsend on the Olympic Peninsula and Keystone on Whidbey Island.

A ferry steams through a passage in the San Juan Islands, one of the most beautiful boat rides in the nation.

Perhaps the premier run of them all is the ferry trip that originates in Anacortes and winds its way through the San Juan Islands with stops on Lopez, Orcas, Shaw, and San Juan Islands. This trip is so beautiful and goes to such a remote part of the state that you sometimes forget it is part of Washington and not a foreign country.

No matter how many times you make this trip, there is always that sense of sailing to far-flung islands. As you leave Anacortes, you see the islands lying low, dark, and green on the horizon and looking as though they form a single land mass. As you draw nearer, you see them as separate islands,

and the ferry goes extremely close to some of them as the deep channel wanders back and forth between the wooded islands.

In addition to the Washington State Ferry system, smaller ferry systems operate in Puget Sound and across the Strait of Juan de Fuca. One runs between Port Angeles and Victoria, B.C. Anyone who has been to that Canadian city will tell

Ferry crewmen stand waiting for the ferry to dock at Orcas Island.

you it is like entering England with all its elegant architecture and formal gardens throughout the provincial capital city. More British than London, some say.

Another ferry connects Steilacoom with Anderson Island (with a stop at McNeil Island, the federal penitentiary). Still another connects Anacortes with Guemes Island.

The state ferry system publishes a free booklet of suggested tours and other ferry information (Seattle Ferry Terminal, Pier 52, Seattle, 98104). Here is a capsulized version to give you an idea of the variety of scenery you can see on day trips or weekend outings aboard the ferries:

Seattle-Bremerton—This trip takes you from downtown Seattle (tour the waterfront first if you have time) across the Sound and through Rich Passage on a 50-minute trip each way. Bremerton offers a tour of the USS *Missouri,* the Naval

Shipyard Museum, the Kitsap County Museum, a drive past remains of the mothball fleet or, as some friends have done, a ferry ride to a good place to shoot pool and have a sandwich and beer before returning to Seattle. From Bremerton you can drive north on the Kitsap Peninsula or south to Gig Harbor and Tacoma across the tall, stunning Tacoma Narrows Bridge.

Mukilteo-Whidbey Island—Whidbey ranks second in offshore islands of the 48 contiguous states with only New York's Long Island larger. Yet much of the slow pace of island life exists, and several of the towns are quite charming. Langley has several false-front buildings, lots of picket

The blockhouse at English Camp on San Juan Island is on one of the prettiest coves on the island. The American Camp is on the windiest and most barren point of the island.

80

fences, and a wide selection of arts and crafts, antique stores, and informal restaurants. Fort Casey State Park, described elsewhere, is another attraction, and the Oak Harbor Air Base near the town of the same name is popular with many visitors. Deception Pass, perhaps the state's most spectacular park, is at the northern tip of the island.

Seattle-Winslow and **Edmonds-Kingston**— These routes are connecting for outings; take one out, the other back. This route takes you to Poulsbo, a Scandinavian settlement with emphasis on Norwegian architecture, murals, and decorations. Several festivals are held there with the Scandinavian influence dominating. Another popular stop is at Port Gamble, a company-owned town (Pope and Talbot Timber Co.) that has been restored to its original appearance. It was patterned after East Machias, Maine, by the founders, and all the homes and other buildings have been painted in Williamsburg colors. A museum in the grocery store has a replica of a sailing ship cabin used by the founders, Victorian furnishings, sawmill artifacts, and Indian baskets. A brochure is available for walking tours of the town.

There are other offerings via the ferries, such as visits to Vashon and Bainbridge Islands, but since all waterfront is privately owned except state and county parks, visitors usually end up driving around the islands and returning to a ferry dock.

The San Juans

Strange how many Washingtonians have never visited the San Juans. It is one of those things we all intend to do but never quite get around to. They are too remote for a day trip, and when one considers the ferry fare plus food and lodging, they can be an expensive trip compared with traveling on the mainland. However, more and more people are visiting the islands on bicycles or going to specific destinations near the ferry docks to avoid the ferry fares for an automobile.

Four major islands are served by the state ferries that depart from Anacortes: Lopez, Orcas,

Shaw, and San Juan. Shaw Island has virtually no tourist facilities beyond a primitive county park. Lopez is the most popular with bike riders because it has few hills. The worst for biking is Orcas, a hilly, even mountainous, island that will put knots in your legs before you get far from the ferry dock.

Islanders have long been almost snobbish about their own island and tend to categorize people according to which island they live on. Once, the more reclusive preferred Lopez, the successfully retired selected Orcas, and artists and writers picked San Juan. But all that is being blended now with a larger influx of all groups to each island. For the visitor, it makes little difference who lives there; it is the scenery that matters.

My family once spent a few weeks on **Lopez,** and I went up there on weekends. They were encamped in a cabin that might best be described as a beach shack. It had tools, beachcombers' treasures, and a good supply of spiders. It had a combination living room, kitchen, and bedroom with a small bathroom and separate bedroom. Firewood was stacked on the porch along with assorted garden tools; the family loved it. They could dig clams on the beach and boil them over a driftwood fire at night with neighbors, and a friend dropped by occasionally with an extra rock cod or two. He also gave us the keys to his boat, which we used to explore the southern rocky end of the island and to perform a minor rescue late one evening when four youths in an antique outboard lost their power in the middle of Mackaye Harbor. The family spent most days going on bike trips or simply poking around on the beach across the road from the cabin.

While there, we had the most fantastic meal we've encountered since coming to the Northwest. We went to Skippers Galley in the town of Lopez, and two of the children ordered a turkey supreme sandwich. The waitress suggested they order only one and share it. They finally agreed, and when it came a few minutes later, it was about a four-decker and almost too much for both. We looked over the menu more carefully after that and found that the chef, who prepares each order individually rather than having four or five orders going at once, offered an omelet for six that took him over an hour to prepare and was bigger around than a large pizza

81

and almost as deep as his turkey supreme sandwiches.

The silence of Lopez Island lulled us as much as the scenery. We had a picnic at a county park and heard absolutely nothing other than the waves lapping on the sandy beach. We saw no other people and dreaded leaving to catch the ferry.

Orcas Island is the mountainous one, complete with Mt. Constitution in **Moran State Park** with a lookout on top of the 2,409-foot peak that offers views across all the islands, most of Washington, and parts of British Columbia. The park also affords numerous good campsites, a lake for swimming and boating, and miles of trails for strolling or hiking.

San Juan Island is a mixture of barren hills on the southern end to dense forest on the northern end. Its moment in history evolves around one of the few wars we've had with a foreign power that involved no human bloodshed. Pig bloodshed, yes. But no human wounds.

It involved the period when nobody knew exactly who owned the San Juans—England or the United States. Both English and American army detachments were stationed on the island. The Americans were at the very southern tip where it is so barren. The English were stationed in a beautiful cove on the northwestern side with lots of trees, sandy beach, water from nearby streams, and shelter from the elements.

An American got extremely angry when he found a pig rooting in his garden that year of 1859, went into the house, and returned with his musket. Result—one dead pig. But, it was an English pig that belonged to the Hudson's Bay Co. The tense situation that developed caused both armies to prepare for battle in what has become known as the

Part of the Hotel de Haro was built in 1850 as a Hudson's Bay trading post. An old lime kiln is at right.

Pig War. No shots were fired, and finally, in 1872, Kaiser Wilhelm I of Germany was called in to arbitrate the boundary dispute. His decision gave the San Juans to the United States.

The west coast of San Juan Island reminds one of the Mendicino Coast of California or some of the more barren islands in the Mediterranean. One of the favorite forms of recreation there is watching killer whales frolic beyond the steep cliffs.

All over the island are rabbits imported decades ago and now virtual dictators of the southern end of the island. Rabbit hunts, some involving hundreds of people, have failed to significantly dent their population, lending credence to the belief that most species grow stronger when faced with threats to their existence. The whole southern end of the island resembles a rabbit warren, and you'll see hundreds, if not thousands, of them while driving along the paved roads past the American Camp to Cattle Point.

At the northern tip is a resort complex called **Roche Harbor.** It includes an ancient hotel, several rental cabins, pool, beaches, playgrounds, a vast marina where sailboats from all over the world dock, and an airstrip where small planes seem to lift the shingles off the cabin roofs when they come in and take off.

This complex once was owned by a family that operated a limestone quarry nearby. The rental cabins were for workers' families, and the hotel was one of the premier resorts in the Northwest. Up in the woods behind the resort is a strange mausoleum built by the Roche Harbor founder, John S.

A fishing boat is tied to a buoy in the San Juans waiting for the tide to change.

McMillin, for his burial place. The mausoleum is round with six limestone pillars supporting a decorative circle. A limestone table in the center represents his family table around which they would symbolically gather in the next world. He had chairs installed for his sons and daughters, which are crypts for their ashes.

Other islands in the group include Decatur, Blakely, Henry, Johns, Spieden, Stuart, Waldron, Patos, Sucia, Matia, Lummi, Sinclair, Cypress, and Guemes, although the latter three are separated from the main cluster and often are not considered part of the San Juans. Guemes is reached from Anacortes by a ferry.

The other San Juans are accessible only by boat or plane, and most have landing strips. Nearly all of Sucia Island is a state marine park, and its long fingers of sheltered water are favorite destinations for boaters on vacation. Charter boats are available ranging from small runabouts to cabin cruisers to yachts complete with crew and cook. And, the best way to view the islands is from a boat because all have small coves where you can stop to camp or stretch your legs far from the nearest crowded resort.

Although the islands are within sight of the mainland and are definitely part of the state and nation, there is still the feeling you are away from all of the rest of civilization. You're not, of course, but it is a nice feeling.

83

Birch Bay

A few years ago friends who owned a house on the beach at Birch Bay decided to have a weekend party before renting it again. They invited perhaps a dozen families, told them to bring food, sleeping bags, tents if they had them, beach clothes, and, if desired, *Frisbees.* Since we had only been through Birch Bay and the weekend sounded like disorganized fun, we accepted.

It was a casual, mixed-up weekend with tiny children wandering through a sea of adult legs in search of parents, food cooked outside over campstoves, on the beach, and even in the kitchen from time to time. Part of our family slept in a tent, two of the girls in the living room, and somebody else upstairs. We were on our own at meal time, and there was inevitably a permanent lineup outside the bathroom.

During the morning we walked out across the broad beach, at least a quarter of a mile at low tide, to the water where we gathered dungeness crab that huddled among the eelgrass and seaweed. Some dug clams, and the children amused themselves by building sand castles or dams across the braided, slow streams of saltwater that followed the tide out to sea. Sunburn became the major problem with children, who could see no reason for putting medicine (sunburn ointment) on themselves before they hurt. Preventive medicine for children is as hard to sell as going to bed early when they're having fun.

In the afternoon we rigged up a volleyball net by propping the poles in the sand like fence posts on a rocky farm and played until the tide came back in about sundown. That night we built a giant bonfire on the beach for marshmallows and hotdogs and talked until we yawned our way back to the sleeping bags.

Parents formed a co-ed volleyball game on the beach at Birch Bay while the children built sand castles.

84

It was an excellent weekend, and we made friendships during those two days that have endured.

Strangely, we don't hear much about Birch Bay, although it is one of the state's most popular summer-vacation towns. Perhaps part of the reason is that the town keeps such control on visitors that those in search of excitement stay away. We were delighted to find one beach town with a street along the water that insisted pedestrians have the right-of-way, and with policemen patrolling the streets constantly to keep them safe so small children can walk to the amusement center without having to be faster than high-school kids in their cars.

As is much of Whatcom County, Birch Bay has become a very popular area for Canadians. During the summer British Columbia license plates vastly outnumber American, and like some Washington residents, many Canadian families reserve the same cabin at one of the courts for a week or even a month summer after summer.

In addition to Birch Bay State Park on the southern curve of the wide, crescent-shaped beach, there are hundreds of cabins for rent each summer. In the town are many resort amenities, such as the amusement park, a roller skating rink, go-cart tracks, a golf course, rental boats, and bicycle rentals.

Deception Pass

Time after time we are drawn back to Deception Pass State Park. If we don't suggest it, our children will. We have gone there on spur-of-the-moment picnics, to show out-of-town visitors Puget Sound away from the cities, and simply because we can't stand the thought of another winter weekend inside the house.

Every time we've gone there, we started at Rosario Beach on the north end of the park, and it never ceases to amaze us how many people that relatively small place can absorb and still leave room for privacy. We still joke about the time we went there and spent the whole afternoon sitting on logs pawing through the small, smooth stones in search of agates. A freighter could have run

This cliff at Rosario Beach, a part of Deception Pass State Park, gives a view across the Sound to the other San Juan Islands and Canada, on a clear day.

85

aground 10 feet away, and we probably wouldn't have noticed it.

Beaches are the best babysitters we've ever found, and not once have we heard a child complain of being bored on the beach, even when the rain was being whipped across the sand. There is a fascination to the beach and the coast that makes one wonder if there isn't something primeval in that attraction.

Such speculation aside, we have come to think of Deception Pass State Park as the ultimate park in our state's park system. It has all those miles of beach and cliff, hiking trails, camping sites, hundreds of picnic areas, wide expanses of lawn for ball games, and some of the best scenery on Puget Sound. So much of the Sound's scenery is low, green land surrounded by water with little variety in the shoreline that the Deception Pass area affords visual relief.

86

Another side of the Rosario Beach peninsula offers rocks to climb on and tide pools to stare into.

Walking across the two-span Deception Pass Bridge is almost guaranteed to give you at least a mild case of acrophobia, especially when the tide is rushing through the narrow passage, swirling in and out of whirlpools far below.

Once we walked down the trail on Goat Island, which divides the pass and the bridges, to the water's edge. The tide was running hard, and we could almost touch one of the whirlpools a few feet off the island. We amused ourselves by tossing sticks into them and watching the sticks spin almost as fast as the spin cycle of a washing machine.

Much of the park was constructed during the Depression of the 1930s by Works Progress Administration and Civilian Conservation Corps workers. They produced stone walls and bridges that today would be too expensive to build.

There are other excellent parks throughout the state, many which we have never visited. Many parks have received so little publicity that it always comes as a surprise to visit a new one and find it excellent by anyone's standards. It is doubtful anyone other than state parks employees have visited each one of the more than 120 parks.

Salmon

I doubt that there are any worse fishermen than me in the state. Although I knew how to fish with a pole, line, hook, and sinker with worms and grasshoppers for bait when I was a child, I have never mastered the more sophisticated gear used now, such as rods and reels. In the two decades I have lived in Washington, I have caught one small salmon, no steelhead, one or two searun cutthroat, perhaps a half dozen Dolly Vardens, and about the same number of rainbow and eastern brook trout. People as inept as me do not place creatures on the endangered list.

Yet some of my most pleasant memories of my first years in Washington involve fishing—yes, even steelheading. When we were first married, we would often get up before dawn and drive to Edmonds or Mukilteo, rent a kicker boat (a 14-foot boat with 20-horsepower motor) from a boathouse, load our rods and reels and flashers and frozen herring, plus coffee and rolls, and take off into the unknown in search of salmon.

Although I was a terrible fisherman, I knew just enough about equipment to be something of a gear snob. I was appalled when my wife chose her salmon rod. It was stiff enough to serve as a mast on a sailboat, and I told her it would never work. She insisted it would and bought it. Of all those

frigid mornings in Puget Sound off the tip of Whidbey Island, only one salmon was caught by our boat, and of course, my wife caught it. My complaints about her rod had to end.

It has never occurred to us since to go out into the Sound early in the morning again. Part of the reason is that we're simply not as brave as we once were, and we don't like the idea of leaving a houseful of orphans. To give you an example of the dangers out there before dawn, sitting in a fogbank, we were drifting with the running tide one morning and heard a steady splashing somewhere in the distance. Soon we realized it was the propeller of a ship that was apparently bearing down on us. But we couldn't tell where the ship was and didn't know which direction to flee. We were afraid to start the motor to escape because then we wouldn't be able to hear the ship coming. So we sat, waiting for it to materialize out of the gloom, my hand on the starter cord. Soon it passed us and kept going south, unseen, down the Sound. We were a bit nervous the rest of the day.

A friend had a similar thing happen to him and another fisherman out in a kicker boat, except they were trolling and didn't hear the ship bearing down on them. The first clue he had that something was wrong came when his partner suddenly looked almost straight upward over the head of my friend, who was seated in the stern. My

A view of Deception Pass taken from the Deception Pass Bridge.

A view of Deception Pass taken from the Deception Pass Bridge.

Rocky shoreline and a sentinel tree mark shore of Puget Sound island.

88

friend looked around and all he could see through the fog were big numbers painted on the bow of the ship. Even though they gunned the motor and got out of the way, he said he still sees those numbers in his dreams sometimes, and it happened more than 25 years ago.

So, there is more to salmon fishing in the Sound than getting up early and hoping the fish will choose your tempting bait. Much more.

Our luck was about the same going after searun cutthroat in Ebey Slough just north of Everett. We launched our inflatable boats without checking the tide tables, and got out into the middle of the slough just in time to catch the incoming tide that twirled us along like corks in a draining bathtub. Finally we were able to lash ourselves to a bridge piling, knowing we were stuck there until the tide ebbed. We didn't catch anything that day, either.

One fishing custom I've never fallen for was opening day. Friends in eastern Washington go out *only* on opening day because it is a social event. They enjoy being crammed in the small lakes—Williams, Fishtrap, or Rock Lake—with boats almost touching each other, lines getting entangled, and being serenaded by three drunks in a cabin cruiser who don't care if the fish bite or not.

For the two years before this book was written (I'm not sure if I'm invited again), I went with some fellow workers on a salmon charter trip at Westport and brought my usual luck along. While others caught the first fish, the biggest, or hooked their limit first to collect the money we'd put into a pot for such luck, I managed to haul up one juvenile salmon the first year and a sea bass the second year. Both came to about $20 a pound figuring all expenses. I'll probably go again if I'm invited, but they've been looking at me with such pity that they may decide they would do me a favor by excluding me.

Still, the urge to fish occasionally is there. We have several sets of specialized fishing gear in the basement—casting reels, spinning reels, salmon reels—that demand use. But, I doubt the fisheries people take my catches into consideration when they build hatcheries or stock the remote lakes.

Wildlife Refuges and Recreation Areas

One September morning I took a gaggle of boys up to Deception Pass State Park for my son's birthday party. While they rambled among the rocks and tidepools to work off the energy stored from the two-hour drive, I fiddled with the campfire to get a bed of coals for their hot dogs. While I was engrossed in this task, an elderly couple strolled up and planted a telescope on a tripod on the bank above me. Both wore binoculars around their necks, and they peered intently along the shore.

They were birdwatchers from Texas. Since his retirement two years earlier they had been traveling the country, following the birds so to speak. They planned to spend at least another three weeks in Washington "birding," with an emphasis on shore birds.

Soon a young man came by with a pair of binoculars as large as those used by Rommel in the North African desert. He lived nearby, he said, and soon he and the Texas couple were comparing notes, talking about species of birds I'd never heard of. I excused myself and went back to coal tending, something I understood.

A few days later I talked to Don Richardson of Washington's tourist promotion division. He said Washington was a birder's paradise. Willapa National Wildlife Refuge, especially on Long Island out in Willapa Bay, had the best birding in the country. More species of birds occupied that refuge than any other in the state, more than most throughout the country.

Although birdwatching is one of those things I keep putting off "until I have more time," like reading *War and Peace,* I feel the same way about wildlife refuges as I do about the wilderness areas I'll never visit: I'm glad they're there. And although I am not a hunter, I can understand the philosophy behind having refuges for birds and game animals such as deer and elk.

One of the most interesting is Turnbull National Wildlife Refuge near Cheney. It was something of an oasis in the hot wheatfields that July. We were astonished at the number of small songbirds that lined the fences and perched on the refuge signs after going for miles without seeing a living thing.

Like many refuges, Turnbull appears designed for bike riding—a far better way to appreciate a refuge than following the marked route in a noisy automobile.

At last count, there were 15 national wildlife refuges in Washington, all part of the Pacific Flyway complex that stretches from Alaska to South America to provide migratory waterfowl with resting places, adequate food and shelter during their migrations. The refuges also provide places for endangered species, such as the subspecies Columbian white-tailed deer, to thrive and increase. (I once visited the Columbian White-tailed Deer Refuge and was amazed at how tame the animals were, grazing side by side with cattle near the road.)

Here's a list of the refuges:

Columbia National Wildlife Refuge—A 28,951-acre refuge in the channeled scablands 50 miles north of Pasco and 10 miles west of Othello. A series of small lakes provide wintering area for more than 100,000 ducks and geese. Hunting and fishing in season; camping available. P.O. Box F, Othello, 99344.

Saddle Mountain National Wildlife Refuge—30,810 acres about 40 miles southwest of Othello within the nuclear reactor control zone of the Hanford complex. Closed to all public use. Administered by the Othello office.

Columbian White-tailed Deer National Wildlife Refuge—5,200 acres for the last remaining populations of the endangered Columbian white-tail deer. Two units. The mainland unit is four miles west of Cathlamet, and the 1,700-acre Tenasillahe Island is on the Oregon side of the Columbia River. Fishing and limited waterfowl hunting. Route 1, Box 376C, Cathlamet, 98612.

Lewis and Clark National Wildlife Refuge—Some 20 islands in the Columbia River run 15 miles in the Lower Columbia below Cathlamet. Waterfowl hunting, fishing and boating permitted. Administered by the Cathlamet office.

Ridgefield National Wildlife Refuge—A 3,000-acre refuge in the Columbia flood plain managed primarily for the dusky Canada goose. Fishing and waterfowl hunting under a controlled program. P.O. Box 457, Ridgefield, 98642.

Washington Islands National Wildlife Refuge—Some 870 islets, rocks and reefs along the

92

coast from Cape Flattery south to Copalis. These inaccessible sites are nesting sanctuaries for cormorants, petrels, puffins, auklets, murres, guillemots, gulls, and oystercatchers. Marine mammals use the islands for resting and feeding. All islands have wilderness status. No hunting, fishing, or visiting. Administered by the Willapa Refuge, Ilwaco, 98624.

Willapa National Wildlife Refuge—17,000 acres encompass the southern portion of Willapa Bay, including Long Island and Ledbetter Point on the Long Beach Peninsula. Waterfowl and archery hunting for deer, bear, and elk. Seven primitive marine campgrounds on Long Island's beaches. Ilwaco, 98624.

McNary National Wildlife Refuge—3,631 acres on the McNary reservoir south of Pasco provide resting area with cultivated foods for ducks and geese. Fishing permitted; hunting on adjacent Department of Game area. Headquarters at P.O. Box 308, Burbank, 99323.

Herds of elk congregate at several feeding areas across the state.

Toppenish National Wildlife Refuge—Still in acquisition process, this will ultimately contain 5,300 acres of marsh, meadows and uplands on Toppenish Creek five miles south of Toppenish. Hunting for upland game and waterfowl. Same management as McNary.

Conboy Lake National Wildlife Refuge—Also in acquisition stage, will contain 9,300 acres five miles south of Glenwood. Important migrating and nesting area. Upland and big-game hunting and waterfowl; fishing. Same management as McNary.

Nisqually National Wildlife Refuge—Ten miles north of Olympia. Total of 3,700 acres when acquisition is completed. The Nisqually River Delta is a major habitat for wildlife and waterfowl. Environmental education is an important function of the refuge. 2625 Parkmont Lane, Building B-2, Olympia, 98502.

Some wild animals, such as this young buck deer, become quite tame in wildlife refuges and national parks, but we should always remember they are still wild and can easily be frightened into attacking.

Dungeness National Wildlife Refuge—573 acres, includes 75 acres of forested upland, the sand spit and adjoining tidelands. Dungeness Spit is one of the longest natural sandspits in the world—it's still growing—and is the only land formation of its kind of North America. Seven miles north of Sequim. Access to spit is by foot trail. Key wintering and spring gathering area for black brant and sea ducks. Beachcombing, fishing, clamming, crabbing, horseback riding are popular activities in addition to birdwatching. Administered from the Olympia office.

San Juan Islands National Wildlife Refuge—A group of 84 islands, islets and reefs in north Puget Sound, most of which are included in the National Wilderness Preservation System. Matia, Turn, and Jones Islands have public use and are managed in cooperation with the state parks system. Other islands are nesting and resting sites for glaucous-winged gulls, cormorants, scoters, murres, guillemots, puffins, auklets,

oystercatchers, and various shore birds. No hunting, and some islands are posted against visiting. Headquarters at the Olympia office.

Turnbull National Wildlife Refuge—15,565 acres contain a series of lakes and marshes with adjacent pine uplands. Six miles south of Cheney. A waterfowl display pool with trumpeter swans; also a five-mile auto tour with both the natural and human history of the area explained. Route 3, Box 385, Cheney, 99004.

In addition to the national refuges, the State Game Department has been slowly acquiring some prime pieces of land throughout the state with both recreational and wildlife values. These are called Wildlife Recreation Areas (WRA) and have proven a boon to anyone enjoying outdoor recreation,

A state employee scatters hay for elk in Oak Creek WRA in the Yakima Valley.

94

whether they be hunters or simply lookers.

At last count the department had more than 30 such areas. Some of the most popular are:

Colockum—This is the largest (115,768 acres) holding of the department, located west of the Columbia River near Vantage. It has Rocky Mountain sheep, mule deer, bighorn sheep, pronghorn antelope, chukar, turkey, pheasant, dove, valley quail, and other species of game birds.

Desert, Potholes and Winchester Wasteway—These three WRAs are also known as the Desert Wildlife Recreation Area, and the three total some 67,000 acres of brush, sand dunes, lakes, and the Winchester Wasteway, which is a drainage canal. Fishing is excellent in the area as well as simply sightseeing because of the high sand dunes that sometimes move in on the seep lakes, snuffing them out of existence. Canoeing in the wasteway is becoming more and more popular as the area gets more attention. It is located between Vantage and Moses Lake east of the town of George.

Nisqually Delta—This famous delta just north of Olympia has been the center of controversy over whether it should be industrialized with a port and railroad yard or preserved in its present state of marshes, winding streams, and tide flats. While the controversy went on, the Game Department went about its business of buying land (651 acres) at the estuary as quietly as it could. Suddenly the department owned some of the most crucial land, which helped preserve it. A plan circulated a few years ago would make the entire Nisqually River from the Nisqually Glacier on Mt. Rainier to Puget Sound a series of parks and preserved landscapes. For the time being, it appears the delta has been saved for wildlife and those who enjoy either watching it or killing it.

Oyhut—This 682-acre preserve, at the southern end of the Ocean Shores Peninsula where Grays River enters the ocean, is known as the best place in the state to see the most birds. Eight kinds of gull, terns, jaegers, sandpipers, hawks, golden plovers, wandering tattlers, whimbrels, willets, black turnstones, loons, scoters, grebes, and the list goes on and on.

Other WRAs include:

Banks Lake (44,702 acres) near Grand Coulee

Gloyd Seeps (7,106 acres) just north of Moses Lake

John's River (1,229 acres) 12 miles southwest of Aberdeen

Olympic (962 acres) 15 miles north of Aberdeen

Crab Creek (17,005 acres) and Priest Rapids (2,501 acres) just east of Beverly

Long Lake (6,020 acres) and Lenora Lake (8,940 acres) near Soap Lake

Sherman Creek (8,068 acres) between Lake Roosevelt and the Kettle Mountains in north-central Washington

Sinlahekin (13,799 acres) just south of Loomis

Shillapoo-Vancouver Lake (1,456 acres) 12 miles north of Vancouver

Klickitat (10,556 acres) between Goldendale and Glenwood

Little Pend Oreille (40,861 acres) 13 miles east of Colville

W.T. Wooten (11,185 acres) 13 miles south of Dayton

Asotin Creek (8,725 acres) and Grouse Flats (680 acres) near Asotin

Skagit (9,619 acres) west of Conway

Quincy (12,759 acres) near Quincy

Stillwater (433 acres) near Carnation

McNary (9,496 acres) near Burbank

Sunnyside (1,684 acres) 35 miles east of Yakima

Entiat (10,883 acres) and Swakane (11,838 acres) just upstream from Wenatchee

Methow (11,669 acres) near Twisp

Chelan Butte (3,170 acres) near Chelan

Scatter Creek (1,080 acres) 18 miles south of Olympia

Lake Terrell (1,051 acres) north of Ferndale

LeClerc Creek (613 acres) in the extreme northeast corner of the state

Wahluke Slope (57,839 acres) on the backbone of the Saddle Mountains east of Beverly

Rattlesnake Slope (3,341 acres) bordering Atomic Energy Commission reservation near Richland

The largest complex of all is composed of L.T. Murray (102,801 acres), Wenas (17,099 acres) and Oak Creek (84,386 acres) stretching along the entire Yakima river between Yakima and Ellensburg. It is world famous for its elk-feeding station during the winters when up to 4,000 elk may visit various feed stations. As many as 2,000 persons a day visit the Oak Creek headquarters to view the elk munching on hay.

Wildlife Viewing

Pacific World Preserve—Nine miles east of Sequim on U.S. 101, near Gardiner. This preserve is called the home of the only remaining buffalo wolves *(Canis lupus nubilus)*. The subspecies almost became extinct as their prime source of food, American bison, was killed off in that great slaughter of the 19th century. Government trappers and ranchers trapped and shot all they could find, but a few remaining wolves were acquired by a Dr. E.H. McCleery of Pennsylvania between 1920 and 1931. Then, he turned over his project to Jack Lynch, who moved the wolves to the preserve near Gardiner. He has some 100 wolves on the preserve now. Open daily 10 a.m. to dusk, weather permitting. Admission.

Olympic Game Farm—About five miles north of Sequim. Most of the animals have been collected for use in wildlife films and some Walt Disney productions. You'll see zebras, polar bears, Roosevelt elk, cougars, Siberian tigers, Kodiak bears, and several other species. Summer: 9 a.m.-7 p.m.; winter: 10 a.m.-3 p.m. Admission.

Northwest Trek—Six miles north of Eatonville on Washington 161. This combination zoo and wildlife refuge is the result of a donation by a Tacoma veterinarian and a large bond issue passed by Tacoma voters. Here deer, buffalo, moose, woodland caribou, beaver, and other animals roam the 400-acre preserve. Visitors are taken on a 5½-mile tour on passenger busses, sometimes yielding the right of way to a lazy buffalo or an irritable bull moose. Unfortunately, animals such as bear and wolves are kept in small pens. Otherwise, it is one of the best such wildlife preserves in the country. Admission.

Seattle Aquarium—Pier 59. One of the most natural aquariums in existence with fish appearing to wander up to view us in our cage. The aquarium drops down below Puget Sound. Sea otters, harbor seals, and other native mammals live in the spacious aquarium, and one of the thrills is looking upward and seeing fish and mammals swimming above. Hours: variable by season. Admission.

A seal swims down for a closer look at children on the other side of the glass at the Seattle Aquarium.

Photos such as this one of a fawn can easily lead to what hunters call the Bambi Syndrome—"Who could kill such a beautiful creature?"

96

Marine Nomenclature

If you were buying your first boat, what would you name it? Would you name it after your wife, daughter, or girlfriend? Or would you name it for something in your past that had a distinct impact on your well being?

Private-boat owners are traditionally more likely to name their boat something whimsical, comical, or downright naughty. Commercial fishermen, who own boats such as these shown at Salmon Bay, are more likely to name their boats more straightforward names. All boats appear to be named something: Who ever heard of a boat with no name?

EAST OF THE MOUNTAINS

THERE aren't many from western Washington who really like the flat lands east of the Cascade Range. It seems featureless, barren, devoid of anything on which to focus your attention. Its vast spaces make some people nervous, giving the indication there are no geographical limits.

I am obviously not among them. I like the wheat country and have visited there when it was bitter cold, when a dust storm hit, when it was almost as hot as Yuma, Arizona, and when the winter wheat had just emerged from its months of being dormant and the whole countryside was a brilliant green.

As my friends and relatives point out from time to time, I would probably starve to death over there. And it is true that I probably would never move there again. But like the Olympic Coast, Puget Sound, and the Cascades, I'm glad it is there, and a visit over there occasionally gives us the variety in life we need.

100

Harvesting wheat is a hot and dirty job, although most combines have air-conditioned cabs today.

Wheat Farming

By nightfall the wind usually drops to a whisper, then to silence, and in the morning when the men return to the fields, there is a sprinkle of dew low in the wheat stalks. The first wind comes up from the southwest, little more than a subtle movement in the air, like a sleeping horse shifting its weight. The sky is usually colorless this early in the morning, promising a hot day with no moisture to hold the dust on the earth.

Early in the summer, and again just before harvest, eastern Washington farmers pull 40 or more feet of rod-weeders behind the big tractors. During the first time or two around the summer fallow, in early morning there is little dust because the miniscule weight of the dew holds it down. What dust does stir hugs the ground and drifts only a few feet before sinking. As the wind rises to its steady pace, the driver will be within the dust cloud blown before the hot and strong wind. The tractor driver's eyes will water and form small mud puddles at the corner of his eyes and down his cheeks, his nose will be clogged, and his lips caked by the acrid, fine volcanic-ash soil.

A view of the Chet and Pearl Bell home with the drill rows showing just after the next year's crop was seeded.

101

The children ran through the wheat stubble in the late September afternoon.

They tell me now that nearly every farmer has an air-conditioned cab on his tractor, and many have radios and tape decks with earphones. Perhaps. But I'm glad I was there before the advent of such refinements. Otherwise, I would be unable to stretch the patience of my children by telling them how difficult it was in what they derisively call "the olden days."

Rod-weeders are relatively simple devices that save wheat farmers thousands of dollars each year. They are square-inch steel rods suspended from wheels, geared to turn opposite to the direction they are being pulled. They slide just beneath the surface of the ground to turn up the weeds so the roots are exposed to the sun to die. It is far cheaper than having the weeds sprayed with poison, faster than hoeing thousands of acres by hand, and dirtier than both.

Those early-summer days are exactly like the previous one, and the next and the next until the summer fallow has been worked and reworked and dried in the sun until it is finer than cornmeal. Farmers race continually against the weeds, which have always grown faster and healthier than anything man plants. For centuries farmers have yearned for a way to market weeds; for decades in eastern Washington they have cursed whoever was responsible for importing the Russian thistle (which dies to become a tumbleweed) and James J. Hill, whose railroad is blamed for importing what is now called Jim Hill Mustard, a fiercely hardy weed. And if you want to watch a wheat-farmer's face turn red, tell him you think morning glories are beautiful plants. He will disagree with varying degrees of intensity because once a morning glory takes root in a wheat field, it takes massive doses of poison, applied over a period of years sometimes, to kill it. You'll be able to spot morning glory settlements from long distances by the spots in fields that have not been cultivated.

So during this time of year the farmer listens to the whine of the tractor gears, the clatter of the tracks, and tells direction not by the sun or landmarks or the stars, but by the direction the wind is blowing. For that wind out of the southwest may fluctuate from a sigh to a storm, but its direction is as constant as a river.

Spring plowing is cold, wet, and monotonous because it takes so long. Wheat harvest is hard, nerve-wracking work. Fall seeding is painstaking, and spring fertilizing with ammonia is smelly and dangerous. But, it is rod-weeding that made the most lasting impression on me.

Sometimes after 10 or 12 hours in the fields, a tractor driver will go to bed at night and see the swirling, dun-colored dust on the back of his eyelids while trying to go to sleep. It is haunting and hypnotic. The driver sits amid a constantly shifting cloud. He watches for the track of the marker wheel which extends far enough beyond the weeders for the right tractor track to follow it on the next round and miss no weeds. It is work at its most simple form and can be pure joy for one who can bear hours of solitude. For one who cannot, it would be maddening.

Often on a calm day, the tractor must be stopped for the dust to settle before the marker can be found. And after a heavy farmer's lunch, the

heat, the full belly, the dust, and the droning tractor produce a soothing effect; and the best thing to do is throw the tractor out of gear, throttle it down to a slow idle, and curl up on the seat for a short nap. Those who have tried to resist this midafternoon letdown have been known to wander all over the fields, sound asleep, with the tractor going wherever it pleases.

Whirlwinds are another by-product of the climate and soil. Up to a dozen may be seen at one time moving across the land in slow, stately dances, reaching several hundred feet into the air, straight as Greek columns. Most are of no consequence and cause no damage other than dirtying clothes hung out on a line to dry or whisking dust and straw into open windows and doors.

Their big brothers—dust storms—are a different matter. Old timers can remember being caught by them in the field and having to use fences to feel their way home. Until a few years ago it was normal for farmers to burn the wheat stubble after harvest. This no longer is done because it

This windmill near Washtucna is reputedly the lowest windmill in the state. It sits in a shallow draw where the wind blows steadily, so there was no need to elevate it.

103

Threshing Bees

The first thing you notice when you go to a threshing bee is that steampowered tractors do not roar. They emit soft, damp chugs, and as you get even closer, you smell the warm lubricating oil and woodsmoke, and feel the first chaff in your hair and eyebrows and itching down your back.

Even though farmers with a good memory will recall how much hard work was involved in threshing grain when they were young—there were no air-conditioned farm machines then—still they are drawn to threshing bees much as mothers are drawn to photo albums of their children. And that is part of the fun of attending the threshing bees held each summer in Washington; joining the farmers who remember and the city folk who wish they did.

The old Case and Rumley, and Hart-Parr, and Bates Steel Mule tractors are hauled to the selected field, usually near a town, and set up just so in front of a stationary thresher with a long belt stretched from the tractor's power-takeoff. Then they're ready for the shocked wheat and oats.

Visitors can join in and pitch the shocks of grain into the thresher while the children get themselves coated with chaff climbing the slippery, dusty strawstack that soon accumulates behind the thresher. Part of the fun for all is having something go wrong so the oldtimers can gather around the wounded part to fix it. These oldtimers are also patient with questios for the uninitiated. They will explain the tractors' power ratings. For example, a tractor may have two ratings, such as 16-40. That means it has 16 horsepower on the drawbar (pulling power) and 50 horsepower on the drive belt, or power take-off.

Although threshers look complicated with all their chains and sprockets and shafts and fans and belts as they shake and rattle and spew out grain and chaff, their basic design is relatively simple and hasn't changed much over the years.

The shocked grain goes into the front end at the separator, a series of rotating teeth that beat the grain from the stalks and husks. The grain drops down to a series of shaking screens that are tilted backward. A fan blows across the screens, removing the husks, straw, and chaff while the heavier grain drops through the screens. Then an auger picks up the grain and transports it out into a bin, into a waiting truck, or onto the ground.

The threshing bees are mini-fairs where local Grange units, youth organizations, and church groups may sell refreshments, books, souvenirs, and food. Some, such as the one at **Toledo,** include an air fair with antique planes and skydivers performing. Programs vary from year to year.

You may find it is difficult to keep track of the threshing bees because none promote themselves very much. They are almost always held at the end of August, or early September, because that is when the grain can be harvested. If you are interested in attending call the towns where they have been held in the past; most have a chamber of commerce. Towns with a history of threshing bees are: **Toledo, Riverside** and **Lynden.**

contributes to dust-bowl conditions, and the stubble gives the soil more body and moisture-holding capacity.

When one who knows eastern Washington—but has left it for the city—thinks of the land east of the mountains, a mild case of claustrophobia often sets in. Here we are surrounded by people, trees, and mountains, not to mention that precious commodity—water. We remember those moonlit nights alone on the farm, or sitting on the lawn after a long day's work, when the lights of a car can be seen for several minutes before the sound of the engine is heard; when the baying of a dog can be heard for five miles. After having experienced this life, that of the city often seems a substitute for life; the difference between butter and margarine.

Elberton

Elberton is alive and well and getting better.

Although the town once was a major farming and ranching community in Central Whitman County during the early part of the century, it began a gradual decline, and its residents voted to disincorporate it a few years ago. Elberton appeared doomed to become a ghost town.

But a group of Washington State University students looking for a project in outdoor recreation and planning found another use for Elberton. Why not restore it to its original appearance, using public funds?

The Whitman County Planning Commission and county commissioners agreed it was a good idea and began acquiring land in and around town. Some of it was up for grabs because the taxes had not been paid. Other plots have been acquired through matching-fund requests. More than 100 acres have been acquired, and the county is negotiating for more.

The town will be restored, not changed. It will be an authentic wheat-country town appearing as it did at its height, complete with the general store. The county will own the store and lease it on a concession basis. The post office, church, and tiny city hall will also be restored, and the county hopes to establish trails to old homesites on the hillside overlooking town.

Coulee Country

We had walked across Grand Coulee Dam, meandered through its powerhouses, and wandered around the area without really appreciating its mass until that evening I stepped out onto the tiny balcony of our motel room and looked at the dam in the hard, summer light. For the first time I realized that those small hills on either side of the dam were actually mountains. The dam is so big it dwarfs the landscape around it. After all, it is taller than a 46-story building, more than 12 city blocks long, and is called the biggest concrete pour in the world. (There are rumors of a larger dam in Russia, but we all know about Russia's claims . . .)

The dam was one of the WPA projects of the Depression 1930s that at the time was frequently referred to as a massive federal blunder. But, like so many WPA projects across the country, it has since proven itself to be an excellent investment.

Originally it was built for two purposes (three if you include jobs in the Depression): to provide hydroelectric power and to turn the central Washington desert into productive farms. Before the dam it was an old joke to say a jackrabbit had to carry his lunch and a canteen just to cross the coulee country, and the landscape was littered with abandoned homesteads, broken windmills, and farm equipment.

But, there was another benefit hardly considered at the time, and that is recreation. Since the dam went in and the irrigation project established, a vast series of lakes developed in the coulee. Hundreds, if not thousands, of smaller lakes also appeared to attract waterfowl and fish and provided places for boaters to play.

The 550-foot manmade waterfall that tumbles over Grand Coulee Dam during heavy runoff periods.

107

All the way south and southeast from Grand Coulee Dam to the Columbia River these lakes exist, and new streams flow year-round. Some, such as the popular Summer Falls, put on a more spectacular show during the early summer at the height of runoff.

This is in addition to the first obvious change made by the dam—the vast **Roosevelt Lake** that stretches from central Washington to the Canadian border, all part of the **Coulee Dam National Recreation Area.** There are more than 25 developed recreation areas on the backwaters of the dam, including a section of the Spokane River that is now slackwater. As with many such manmade lakes in the West, this one is notable for the lack of water reaching the soil surrounding the lake. Water in an almost desert landscape makes the surrounding area especially attractive on those hot summer days when heat waves bend and distort the views.

South from Grand Coulee is the series of federal and state recreation areas that total about 40, ranging from **Banks Lake Wildlife Recreation Area** to **Summer Falls State Park** to the **Potholes Wildlife Recreation Area, Desert Wildlife Recreation Area** to the **Saddle Mountain National Wildlife Refuge.** Scattered all through the area are the "pothole" lakes ranging in size from a middle-class family's swimming pool to small lakes. These have been created by water seeping across bedrock and nonporous layers of soil until it emerges into a depression.

These lakes, and the conditions that create them, are one of the unknown developments that resulted from the irrigation system in the Columbia Basin. When the Bureau of Reclamation began the project, such conditions weren't considered and were not a prime worry. The primary consideration was putting water on the soil to make crops grow. What to do with the water after it was used was another, less important subject.

Water picks up natural salts and other minerals from the soil as it flows through. Unless the saline water keeps flowing, it can make the soil totally unproductive and the only recourse is laying drain tile beneath the surface, as they've had to do in much of the south-central California land.

This creates problems for the farmers but doesn't have much effect on recreation, other than rendering some of the water undrinkable. Generally, the salts and other minerals from the soil become nutrients for fish, and some of the largest fish in that part of the state are caught in these lakes. One is Lake Lenice on the lower Crab Creek near Beverly. There are dozens of others that yield fat, healthy fish in the undrinkable water.

More land is expected to be added to the irrigation project as federal funds become available, at least another half-million acres, and that will mean more seep lakes, or potholes, and more drainage streams called wasteways that make excellent canoeing, as does the **Winchester Wasteway** now.

And it may result in another bonanza a Bureau of Reclamation official told about. A rancher who wasn't interested in irrigation gradually found himself the owner of a lake when the project began because a large piece of his ranch was on low ground. The lake kept growing until he had to move some buildings. He wasn't at all happy and was saying unkind things to the government officials. But after awhile he stopped saying them. His unwanted lake became a resort complex, and he earned more money at that for working less than he had as a rancher.

Soap Lake

People still reserve rooms in hotels at Soap Lake in order to bathe in the lake, we are told. A recent insert in a brochure from Soap Lake extols the virtues of the lake water:

"Chemicals in Soap Lake water are effective in producing elimination, stimulation of bile flow, and restoring an alkaline balance in the body. In addition, there is abundant stimulation of perspiration and cleansing of the skin. These qualities are in themselves the solution of many rheumatic and skin troubles, eczema, neuritis, arthritis, sciatica, lumbago, stiffness, muscular pains and nervousness, and also many forms of digestive and intestinal disturbances. Many people drink Soap Lake mineral water. It is easily assimilated by the body supplying necessary

minerals. The water is also beneficial for all kinds of circulatory disorders. For those wishing to take the hot mineral baths, facilities are available. It is also piped into many of the hotels, motels, and homes. Soap Lake water is the only known treatment to arrest Buerger's disease."

A chemical analysis of the lake water yielded 20 different minerals present with high counts of carbonate, bicarbonate, chloride, sulphate and sodium.

In the mid-1950s the lake was faced with a potential threat. Fresh water from the Columbia Basin Project was beginning to enter the lake and alter its unique chemical composition. M.R. Newell, mayor at that time, went to Congress and got the Bureau of Reclamation to drill a ring of wells around the lake to intercept the fresh water. The grateful town erected a plaque for Newell, praising his action for "preserving the salinity of Soap Lake water and its curative qualities for future generations."

110

Dry Falls

During the Ice Age the continental ice sheet moved south of Canada and blocked the Columbia

Summer Falls was created when the Columbia Basin Project's irrigation system was installed.

River in the canyon where Grand Coulee Dam now stands. The river was forced southward across the lava plateau and scoured out some of the coulees we see today. Two major falls resulted, one near Soap Lake and the other at **Dry Falls,** an 800-foot drop that was more than three miles wide, compared with the 165-foot drop of Niagara Falls and only one mile wide.

When the ice sheet receded, the river resumed its normal course, leaving only the etched coulees and a small lake at the bottom of Dry Falls.

An interpretive center overlooks the chasm and vividly tells the story of the falls and the entire Coulee Country.

In the same area are two other features of interest. The **Lake Lenore Caves** are reached by a trail about 10 miles south of the **Dry Falls Interpretive Center.** The caves were formed by the melt waters from the Ice Age and used by prehistoric man as shelter. Only a few artifacts have been found in the caves, such as scrapers, indicating they were used only as temporary shelter.

Near **Blue Lake,** also south of Dry Falls, is a mold of a small rhinoceros in the lava. Called the "Blue Lake Rhino," it is believed to have been lying already dead in a small pond when molten lava flowed into the lake and formed around the body, cooling in the water before it consumed the corpse.

The Columbia Basin Project produced one of the most important waterfowl breeding grounds in the Northwest, as well as resting and feeding places along the migratory route, the Pacific Flyway. Game birds were imported—the Chinese pheasant called "Chinks," chukar, and Hungarian partridges—while native species such as sharptail and sage grouse have declined as their desert and prairie habitat was replaced by the lakes and potholes.

Some of the species using the basin are Caspian terns, which nest on an island in Priest Rapids Pool, ringbilled gulls, Brewer's yellow-headed and red-winged blackbirds, meadowlarks, kildeers, horned larks, and a host of ducks such as ringnecks, canvasbacks, blue and green-winged teal, baldpates, shovelers, pintails, and goldeneyes.

The early Seattle photographer, Asahel Curtis, had an artist retouch one of his photographs to show the vast waterfall that fell over Dry Falls during the Ice Age.

The Flood

fter geologists established that the Ice Age created the system of coulees and dry waterfalls in central Washington, they also more or less blamed the Ice Age and volcano eruptions and lava flows through fissures for creating the dominant landscape of that area.

But there was one stretch of geography that continued to disturb some geologists: the area now known as the Channeled Scabland. Why, right in the middle of a rich farming area, should there be a gouge in the deep soil with "ship rocks" protruding upward from barren canyon floors? Most geologists were content to associate it with the familiar Ice Age and water erosion sources they had come to accept as certified history.

Not so J. Harlen Bretz, a geology professor at the University of Chicago. During a summer excursion to Washington in the 1920s, Bretz was struck by the unusual characteristics of the area. He noted that the scablands begin roughly in the Spokane Valley and run unevenly southwest the length of the state to the Columbia River. This area is marked by what appears to be a series of dry stream beds, cataracts of varying heights, and steep basaltic buttes rising above the rolling, curving wheatfields. The buttes are generally

pointed in a north or northeast direction with the northern end dropping off abruptly. The southern end usually has a more gentle incline, often with crops planted all the way up the slopes to the scabrock that juts out at the top. From the air, Bretz noted, the buttes have a boat shape, sharper at the north than the south end.

In 1965, 42 years after he first propounded his revolutionary theory on the channeled scabland, Bretz received a telegram that ended with the magic words:

"We're all catastrophists."

"During all those years I was fighting for my professional career," Bretz told me a few years ago in an interview when he was 89 years old.

His mistake? He advanced, in 1923, the theory that the scablands were formed by a catastrophic event, or perhaps a series of such events rather than

This dry canyon near Palouse Falls State Park is an example of the canyons and ship rocks carved by the catastrophic floods at the end of the Ice Age. The theory got J. Harlan Bretz in hot water, but after years of debate, his detractors became his disciples.

adhering to the accepted formula of eons of normal erosion activities by the wind and water.

"One summer I was out in Spokane and I saw a section of a topographic map of what we now call the Channeled Scabland, and that map gave me the idea," he said.

He believed the area was created by a catastrophic flood that originated from a vast lake at the site of Missoula, dammed by earth and ice. When the Ice Age waned, the dam broke in one huge flood of Noah proportions, sweeping the land bare of topsoil, scouring out hundreds of canyons and coulees, eventually emptying into the Columbia River at Wallula Gap. The mountains along the Columbia were high enough to swing the flood westward down the gorge through the Cascades and out into the ocean.

Bretz believed the flood headed due east from Missoula across Idaho's panhandle, where it created the lakes that remain today, rushed on down the Spokane Valley, then swung south and slightly west, spreading as it went. It narrowed again as it approached the Snake and Columbia Rivers, and changed the course of the Palouse River. Bretz found evidence that the Palouse originally went down the Washtucna Coulee, where the towns of Washtucna and Kahlotus now stand, and emptied into the Snake some 70 miles farther downstream than it does today.

His theory included the probability of a series of such floods down the same course as the Missoula dam would reform itself with the ebb and flow of the Ice Ages. Each time, it would break again, causing the flood. But he never pressed this possibility as much as he did his basic theory.

The theory went completely against the contemporary geologic thought. Most geologists subscribed to the theory that had evolved during the 19th century in opposition to the strict religious version of creation given in the Bible. All geological formations, the previous thinking went, were the result of catastrophic events, like Noah's flood. Slowly geology gained headway by offering proof that events occurred over long periods of time. By the first of this century, the idea of eons was widely accepted and the catastrophic theory was not.

Then along came Bretz with his catastrophic theory after the profession had worked so hard to refute that line of thinking. Yale and Harvard,

113

which considered themselves the seat of power in geology, were not thrilled. One professor called the University of Chicago "that western trade school" in a paper refuting Bretz.

But, they picked the wrong man to fight. Bretz would not be intimidated. For the next several summers he worked in eastern Washington, going on numerous field trips, gathering ammunition for the battle. He published papers, and papers were published by his opponents, which included most of his profession.

In the summer of 1952 Bretz met George Neff, a geologist and soil specialist with the Columbia Basin Reclamation Project, which then was just entering the irrigation business.

"I started working on the project in 1946," Neff said, "and I started searching the literature on the area to find out what had gone on before so I could understand what to expect now. I ran into the widely divergent theories of the geological history.

"In order to find out what to expect beneath the earth's surface, I had to know how it was put together. I had to know these things so we could know how excess water from the irrigation canals would flow, where to expect seep lakes to form and where to expect the water to flow underground, and so forth. The only thing that seemed to work was Bretz' theory.

"In the summer of 1952 he came out with H.T.U. Smith, a geologist from the University of Kansas. Bretz brought him along as a sounding board for his ideas—someone to bounce them on so he'd know if he was on the right track. Since I had done a lot of digging in the area for soil samples,

There are a series of small waterfalls above Palouse Falls, such as this one in the scabrocks on private land. The Old Mullan Road runs near this section of the river.

Bretz asked me to show him what I had found."

In 1956 a paper appeared under the trio's names offering further proof that the flood theory was sound. Neff's name was on it, too, although he insists it was generosity on Bretz' part to include it.

During all those years Bretz continued teaching and building up a core of disciples—former students, geologists such as Neff who had no academic axes to grind, and a few geologists who weren't committed to the eons theory. But, it was still another 11 years before Bretz had his final day in court. During the 1965 International Geophysical Year in Denver, Bretz was unable to attend because of poor health but had some disciples with enough prestige to arrange a geological trip west from Denver.

The group went by chartered bus across the Rockies to Missoula. At Missoula, a Bretz follower began a lecture illustrated by the scenery outside the bus window and an occasional stop for a hike. All the way across Idaho and along the Columbia River to grand Coulee the group heard and saw the theory explained in minute detail.

From Grand Coulee the bus swung back east across the scabland toward Kahlotus, Washtucna, Hooper, and on into Pullman for the night.

It was in the Kahlotus-Washtucna area that the pieces of Bretz' puzzle all fell into place. The geologists saw the evidence that convinced them: dry cataracts where flood waters once flowed, the rerouting of the Palouse River, the stream beds that never in the memory of man had running water, ripple marks high on canyon walls, and the other clues of great significance to the trained eye.

On that day Bretz' opponents, some of whom had been quite sharp and personal in their disagreement, began eating crow. Some wrote scholarly papers later offering apologies for their previous words. Bretz was finally successful not only in having his theory accepted, he also managed to swing the geological pendulum back toward the center between the eons line of thinking and the catastrophic events.

"It was that last leg of the trip that did it," Bretz said. "And I knew the fight was all over when I received a long telegram of congratulations from the group in Pullman. At the very end were the words:

"We're all catastrophists."

114

Three Forks Pioneer Village

This village on some land of marginal farming value is the outgrowth of a hobby Roger Rossebo has had since a teen-ager. He began collecting bits and pieces of old farm equipment and soon graduated to entire buildings from towns that were being inundated by backwaters of the Snake River as dams were built.

Rossebo has a small town with a general store and all the scales, cash registers, and stocked shelves; a millinery "shoppe" with clothing and manikins; a one-room schoolhouse built of logs, with chairs and desks.

Outside he has a collection of tools, wooden logging skids, sulky rakes, and a whimsical cemetery out back.

The museum is open April through September on Sundays. Arrangements may be made for visits Monday through Saturday by appointment. It is about six miles from Pullman. Take Washington 17 past the Albion Road one mile and turn left. Drive two miles to Merry Mount Stables, turn right onto a gravel road, and drive 2.8 miles. The Rossebo farm and village are on the right side going north.

Address: Three Forks Pioneer Village, Route 1, Box 290, Pullman, 99163.

115

Steptoe Butte

In the midst of the rolling hills of Whitman County's famed **Palouse Country,** another hill or two make little difference, and it is easy to drive past Steptoe Butte, a few miles south of Rosalia on U.S. 195, without noticing anything to distinguish it from the other hills in the area.

But **Steptoe Butte,** modest as it appears, is a geologically important natural feature. It is the 3,613-foot tip of a mountain protruding above the bedrock of basalt that flowed from fissures in eastern Washington during a 10 to 15 million-year span during the late Miocene and early Pliocene eras, accumulating to more than 6,000 feet deep in places.

After the lava flows ceased, the prevailing southwest wind blew in the topsoil that has made the Palouse hills the richest wheat farming area in the world. This wind-blown soil, or loess, also accumulated into incredibly deep thicknesses, often in excess of 40 feet.

But Steptoe Butte remained above the lava and soil, a granite mountain surrounded by other, more recent types of rock, that once was a part of the Selkirk Range. As a result, throughout the world any other such peak is known among geologists as a "steptoe," when a peak of an older composition protrudes above more recent geological material.

The peak, a battlefield nearby, and the small town near it were named for Col. E.J. Steptoe, who was defeated in 1858 by Indians during the series of skirmishes in eastern Washington during the Indian Wars.

Some 30 years later, an Englishman named James Davis (better known as Cashup for his demands that all business in his store be conducted on a cash-up-front basis only) built a magnificent, square two-story hotel with a balcony all around the roof on top of Steptoe Butte. He was convinced it would become a tourist mecca for its aerial-like view of the rolling Palouse Hills. And to decorate the hotel in the regional fashion, Davis hung wheat stalks by the thousand upside down in the lobby,

This winter view from atop Steptoe Butte shows the wind-sculpted Palouse Hills, the richest wheat farming land in the world.

and filled vases, jugs, fruit jars, cups, and drinking glasses with heads of wheat.

Alas, none of this worked, and the hotel was visited only by curiosity seekers, and it was a white elephant on a hill when he died in 1896. A son tried to keep it open, but it burned in 1911.

The family that bought the butte donated it to the state for a park, and today there is a road leading to its crest that winds around and around the butte past a small picnic area. The top is not especially inspring. It bristles with radio and television antennas placed there because of its elevation by various public and private agencies. However, by turning one's back on the shacks and antennas, the view across the Palouse Country is one usually limited to those in a helicopter.

The best times for visiting the butte, and taking photographs, are in the early morning and late afternoon when the low sunlight gives definition to the landscape below and when the air is usually freer of dust.

Old Mullan Road

Occasionally as you drive across the far eastern edge of the state, you'll cross the Old Mullan Road, and about the only hint you have of its existence is a highway marker or local historical society sign. It was started in 1858 when Lt. John Mullan was assigned to survey a road between Fort Walla Walla and Fort Benton in north-central Montana, which was the head of riverboat navigation. As Indian troubles increased, the Army felt a need for a road between the two forts for both supplies and strategic use. But the Indians objected to it, and the Army yielded to their pressure until peace of sorts was reestablished. The road was begun in 1858. It went north from Fort Walla Walla to present **Lyons Ferry State Park,** where the Palouse empties into the Snake. It crossed the Snake just downstream from the Palouse, and followed the Palouse across the broken land and crosses Washington 26 a few miles

Those Trap Wagon Blues

For three summers this battered old truck defeated my attempts to coax it into operation. I show it here in hopes it will be the last word, and that the last word will be mine.

They are called "trap wagons" and are used on wheat farms to haul diesel, gasoline, tools, grease, oil, and whatever else might be needed for work in the fields.

One newcomer to the wheat country innocently called them "crap wagons," and more than one farmer agreed the tenderfoot had a point.

The photo was taken during a fall visit to the wheat country with storm clouds moving in. The door was left open, not by accident but because it makes no difference if the rain and snow get inside or not. For all I know, it was left out in the middle of the field two or three miles from the house all winter.

east of Washtucna near Hooper. If you'll stop at the historical marker, you can see the old road running along the rim of the hill on both sides of the highway. From there, it went through Benge and on north through the lake country south of Spokane and swung eastward across the top of Idaho and into Montana. It was used, but not very much, until the railroads appeared in the 1880s.

Occasionally local riding clubs, or loosely associated groups of horsemen, form an expedition to retrace portions of the road. Inquire locally for information.

Lyons Ferry State Park, at the conjunction of the Palouse and Snake Rivers.

Garden in the Rocks

Scattered throughout arid eastern Washington are thousands of rock outcroppings that serve no useful purpose other than breaking up the generally treeless, rolling landscape. To most farmers and cattle ranchers the rocks are a waste of land; they have to pay taxes on rocks.

Herman Ohme didn't agree. In 1929 he purchased a small fruit orchard four miles north of Wenatchee overlooking the Columbia River. Included in the deal was a high rocky point that would grow only sagebrush and desert grass—certainly not fruit trees.

But Ohme liked the barren spot because of its magnificent views of the Columbia River, the Cascade Mountains, and the Wenatchee Valley with its world-famous fruit orchards. Ohme decided he would build a home there.

In preparation for that day, he began landscaping the drab rocks and pumping water up from the valley below. He brought in evergreen trees from the nearby Cascades and added low-growing alpine plants and prostrate junipers. With these he mixed plants such as phlox cublata, dryas, veronicas, campanulas, dianthus, yuccas, thyme, cactus, native ferns, and many varieties of sedum.

After 10 years the fascinating hobby grew beyond his early expectations and began attracting many visitors, not only from Washington but from all over the West. Gradually the garden's fame grew until in 1939 Ohme officially opened the gardens to the public.

The Ohme family has continued developing the gardens and each year expanded them a little more until they now cover 10 acres.

To reach the gardens, drive north from Wenatchee on U.S. 2 and 97 about four miles, where signs near the intersection of the highways will lead you directly to the gardens.

Visitors are welcome from 8 a.m. until dark seven days a week from early April until late in October. There is an admission charge. Children under 12 are admitted free if accompanied by an adult.

SEATTLE

Dozens of types of boats can be seen on Green Lake at any time of the year.

ADVENTURES in Seattle appears last but not because it is necessarily the best part of the state or because I wanted to emphasize it. Instead, I found myself procrastinating because Seattle is the most difficult to write about. Working on a newspaper keeps one so close to a city that it sometimes is difficult to separate what is written about it daily from what the reader might not know.

Seattle gives a sense of well-being, which a visit to other cities will enforce. This sense of well-being is responsible, I believe, for the lack of truly regional literature. We have what amounts to a Northwest school of poets, and one of painters to a certain extent. But not in fiction. The Northwest has produced no Steinbecks, no Faulkners, no Sinclair Lewises. My thesis, stated several times before, is that the Northwest has no real problems connected with its geographical location. Life is quite mild here and always has been. While it is true we have had our labor problems and our romances with forms of government other than democracy, still the tame seasons and the rain seem to rinse these problems away.

A Special City

What can you say about a city you love without sounding like a boastful, boring parent among a group of childless couples? Even on the evening this is being written, with the rain settling on the city like a leaden fog, Seattle is such a great city in comparison with all others I know about that I can only sigh in exasperation and think about the trip to the tip of Baja California next month. Whenever we visit a different climate, I always catch myself thinking of its advantages over Seattle and the possibility of moving there one day. But we never have and probably never will.

We like the Bend, Oregon area, but we are too accustomed to the salt-water here, and our son is in the Sea Explorer Scouts. We enjoyed a week in Tucson a few years ago, but the spiders and rattlers and lack of skiing within an hour's drive made it less attractive. We loved the Balearic Islands off

122

Spain, but knew a few months spent there would be an exercise in homesickness for all the things we take for granted here. We like the climate of the northern California Coast (anywhere from Santa Barbara north) but cannot get over the idea that California is a little crazy. Some of the Pacific Islands appeal, especially Hawaii, but the islands are too lush, too restrictive.

Apparently we are content. If nobody has conducted a study of Seattle residents in this age of mobility, they should. When the city went through an employment crisis in the late 1960s, and people with graduate degrees were standing in unemployment lines reminiscent of the 1930s bread lines, one aspect of the situation was seldom mentioned: There were jobs for them elsewhere in the country, or even in foreign countries, but it never occurred to many of them to leave Seattle. It was unthinkable.

A view from Gasworks Park in Seattle shows sailboats and power boats cruising between Lake Union and Lake Washington.

Interestingly, many of those highly trained—overqualified, if you will—people now are busy at lines of work they never thought of going into before it was forced on them. Some build wooden rowboats. Others own small stores. They are in a variety of trades all over the Puget Sound area, and they have graduate degrees in engineering and the sciences. But they're still here.

True, Seattle has a way of irritating its citizens occasionally. It simply had to build that concrete river through the heart of the city, demolishing some fine neighborhoods and rendering others virtually uninhabitable. If the original freeway planners had gotten away with it, many more square miles of the city would be under cement. It would be only a place for commerce, not for living. It would be controlled even more by absentee landlords than it is now.

But something happened in the 1960s. Perhaps it was an outgrowth of the environmental movement combined with the thousands who took to the streets to oppose the Vietnam war. Whatever it was, more and more citizens of the city demanded that the city remain a decent place to

123

live. While the landlords make the money today, it wasn't the landlords who pushed to have Pioneer Square restored to its original importance in the city. It wasn't the bureaucrats who wanted to preserve the Pike Place Markets, nor did they instigate the creation of tiny little parks all over the city where vacant lots and triangles at intersections once collected litter. In all these and other cases, it was the citizens. And it was usually only a few who got the rest of us interested.

Thus, you will find residential areas within walking distance of town. You will find houseboats still bobbing on Lake Union and Portage Bay instead of concrete piers, platforms, condominiums, and apartment buildings along every square foot of shoreline. It took the threat of seeing the shores of Lake Washington virtually vanish beneath boat docks and patios to startle us into action.

A few years ago when we began working on *The Seattle GuideBook,* one of our plans was to list every tiny neighborhood park in Seattle and boast of them a bit. But, we met kindly opposition when we began collecting the material. We were told the

parks are intended primarily for the residents within walking distance, and it would be appreciated if we didn't call attention to them. Some might be considered better than others, and people from other areas might flock in and take them over. There is nothing discriminatory about this, we were assured. It was just that each neighborhood had its own parks, and it would be best for all if they were allowed to exist without publicity.

Thus, we were charmed into pretending something didn't exist. On the other hand, there are all the other parks to point out—Green Lake, Lincoln, Gasworks, Freeway Park, Waterfront Park, the Burke-Gilman Trail from Seattle to Bothell, and so forth. And, of course, Seattle Center itself, probably the grandest legacy of a World's Fair in any city that has ever hosted the fair.

124

One of the most popular spectator sports in Seattle is watching boats going through the Hiram Chittenden Locks, commonly known as the Ballard Locks.

It is impossible to take the Seattle Center for granted, even though it has been there since 1963. It has such quality, such class that nobody is opposed to its activities, its greenery, its museums, and activity buildings. It is one of our showplaces that the city wants people to use, rather than simply admire. There is none of the look-but-don't-touch nonsense there, no "Keep off the grass" signs.

When we have out-of-town guests, we tend to confuse them with alternatives for recreation. They want a restaurant with a view, for example. A view of what? we ask. The Sound? The city? One of the lakes? The mountains? The skyline? The Ballard Locks?

They want a quiet afternoon. Seattle Center? Freeway Park? The waterfront? A ferry ride? Which museum?

They want to try an ethnic restaurant. Japanese? Chinese? Vietnamese? French? Italian? Lebanese? Mexican?

Before our guests' first evening is over, we're unintentionally sounding like paid boosters of the city, so we temper it by warning them they should have rain gear with them. Don't get caught on either of the Lake Washington floating bridges in rush hour. Watch driving on the hills downtown if you're not accustomed to a car with a stick shift.

A climactic scene from Wagner's "Das Rheingold," **125** *during the annual Pacific Northwest Festival in which Wagner's entire "Ring" cycle is performed in German and English.*

When our cultural life is brought into the conversation, we try to keep it casual when we mention that our symphony has no problems raising money and that it is giving more and more concerts each year. We speak of the Pacific Northwest Festival, then explain that it is Wagner's "Ring" Cycle performed here each summer in both German and English. Yes, it does attract Wagner fans from all over the world. Our Art Museum is world famous for its Oriental art collection. The Seattle Repertory Theater is one of the finest such theaters in the country and plays almost consistently to full houses. We don't have a major dance company here, we apologize, but we do have dance companies. We have a Northwest school of poetry, a legacy of the late Pulitzer Prize winner, Theodore Roethke and his talented, generous disciple, Nelson Bentley, and David Wagoner, one of the nation's most respected poets. We have a number of major prose writers living in the area, but no, we don't really have a Northwest school of fiction.

But most of all, perhaps, Seattle offers a way of living known to few other cities. There is a remarkable absence of social pressure, and an equally remarkable amount of personal freedom. Few things are more frustrating to newcomers with an illustrious family tree than trying to impress Seattle people simply on the basis of their birth. Royalty, real or imagined, doesn't count for much in Seattle. After all, when members of some of the wealthiest and most powerful families in the Northwest drive old cars, live modestly, and choose their friends on the basis of companionship values rather than income, it clearly isn't the place a publisher of a social register could hope to make much money.

Seattle reflects what is good and bad about the state as a whole. But the good still far outweighs the bad. Living in Seattle offers more variety in ways of life than many so-called major cities. Not only are its metropolitan standards high (meaning it is being redesigned constantly to make it more pleasant for its residents), it is one of the most convenient places in America for the physically active to live. Puget Sound, the ocean less than three hours away by car, the mountains less than an hour away, rivers and lakes, farms, small towns with their personalities still intact, a mild climate with infrequent major storms, no poisonous snakes . . . Enough. It sounds too good to be true.

Rather than giving a complete rundown on what Seattle offers (we've already done so in *The Seattle GuideBook*), here is a list of major areas of the city that contribute to its diversity and interest:

Waterfront—Only a short time ago the waterfront, except for about two blocks, was strictly business. There were a cluster of restaurants and a few other places of business for

Pier and dock fishing is a popular pastime in Seattle, and several places have been set aside especially for the sport. This group tried their luck at Duwamish Head in West Seattle.

visitors, and that was it. Now the whole waterfront from the downtown area north to Pier 92 on the edge of Magnolia is available to the public. Import stores, restaurants, Waterfront Park, Aquarium, the complex of shops, cafes, and restaurants at Pier 70, and north of there a strip park for walkers, joggers, and bikers. It is now very much a people place with enough maritime business remaining to give it a definite waterfront character.

Pike Place Markets—This shopping area, seemingly clinging to a hillside by its fingernails, is dear to the heart of traditionalists in Seattle. It has a farmer's market, ethnic restaurants, hippie businesses, and all the sights, smells, and uneven floors that go with it. At one time the city fathers were intent on "rehabilitating" the markets and turning them into an area as sterile and exciting as a hospital kitchen. Tempers heated up among the intelligentsia, and the bureaucrats' plans cooled. The markets remain more or less as they were— marvelously tacky, so unconcerned with class that they have their own class. It is a great place for out-of-town visitors to wander an hour or two. They'll never get bored, and neither do locals.

Pioneer Square—This was the heart of Seattle at one time. After the great fire of 1889 leveled the downtown district, the merchants wisely rebuilt of stone and brick. But the business district slowly migrated to the north, and Pioneer Square became a prototype for Skid Roads across the nation. (We must repeat again that the term, Skid Road, originated there when Henry Yesler, a pioneer merchant and sawmill owner, used what is now Yesler Way to skid logs down the slope to his sawmill, hence Skid Road). After the Skid Road atmosphere clung to the area for several decades, some businessmen with a Cassandra-like vision into the future began reclaiming the elegant old buildings and installing offices for designers, architects, and even a banking magazine. Gallery owners followed, then chic restaurants, boutiques, bookstores, and artists. Soon there was a battle on to preserve the area and prevent demolition squads from coming through with their cranes and wrecking balls and plans for concrete-and-glass structures to replace the old buildings. The wreckers were defeated, and the area is now one of Seattle's showplaces. And Pioneer Square, a tiny park at a major intersection, isn't even a square. It is a triangle.

International District—Most major West Coast cities have what they collectively call Chinatown, even though it also has residents of Japanese, Filipino, Caucasian, and even English and Swedish extraction. In Seattle the area is a bit less restrictive by title and is called International. Here, near the Kingdome, are restaurants, grocery stores, gift shops, and storefronts decorated in Oriental and South Pacific designs. As with other key areas in Seattle, there was a threat of progress hanging over the district for several years as developers wanted to move in and modernize it. But cooler heads prevailed, and the area remains intact. Some of the best, and least expensive, eating is available there in all of Seattle.

The Seattle Center's Folklife Festival brings music and dance from all over the world each year, including belly dancers such as this one.

127

City Walking

Every September we experience something of a recreational lag—school starts and everything else stops. Weekend trips don't work because at least one of the children has plans for the weekend—volleyball practice, studying for a test, or whatever. We become so accustomed to getting our exercise out of town that we always have to readjust to urban experiences, even though all the major cities of Washington and many of its small towns have established walking and bike trails for such activities.

It is all part of a plan—almost revolutionary—to make cities decent places to live rather than just places to work. It has resulted in Washington and several of its cities being admired or envied by publications from other parts of the country proclaiming this area as the most "livable" in the country. The pity is that the rest of the country isn't following us at a faster rate.

For specific example, the day I'm writing this is one of those beautiful winter days with a clear sky, crisp air, and all the temptations it offers. It is a tough day to be a writer because there are places we could go on this Sunday afternoon that we haven't visited for several months. The temptation is to load up anyone who wants to go and head for the ferry dock. We could ride across to the Kitsap Peninsula, drive north to **Port Gamble** and **Port Townsend,** cross on another ferry to **Fort Casey State Park,** a place dear to the heart of our war-story reading son, drive down Whidbey Island and catch the ferry back to Edmonds and be home before dinner time.

"With so many things to do that cost so little," said a writer friend from the Midwest, "I don't see how you find the time to write."

A stop in the Museum of History and Industry is a good way to get warm after a hike along the Foster Island trail.

128

So it is in Washington. Anyone with good health who complains of being bored should be shipped off to Dalhart, Texas, or some such inland address.

On those fall or winter afternoons (this one excepted), we usually pack up a few snacks, wear comfortable walking shoes, and drive fewer than 15 minutes for a walk.

One such walk that is always interesting because of the people factor is around **Green Lake,** almost within sight of our house. When the city council purchased the lake for a park back around the turn of the century, there was an uproar of major proportions among the citizens. "The lake is so far out in the wilderness that nobody will ever use it," they said. They were wrong. At that time it became fashionable to ride a trolley to Green Lake, which took quite some time, enjoy a picnic and a swim, then ride back through the tall timber to the city. Remember that at this time bear were still being killed along the shores of Lake Washington and that Everett was as far away, all things considered, as Walla Walla is today.

Today Green Lake is virtually in the middle of the city, but it is surrounded by a large green belt laced with walking and biking paths. The lake has been developed only enough for swimming areas to be established and rowboats and paddleboats to be rented. In one afternoon you can see kayakers practicing their skills, including the tricky Eskimo roll, paddleboats with half a dozen kids hanging onto them, inflatable boats of every description, sailboats heeled over on one pontoon, canoes, radio-controlled and noisy toy hydroplanes, infrequent midget hydroplane races, dogs swimming with great exuberance after sticks, runners and joggers of all ages and descriptions, bike riders, bathing beauties (and some not so beautiful), family picnics, dog walkers, baby walkers, occasional neckers, and so forth. All this along a 2.8-mile trail along a lovely lake with its full complement of begging ducks and nagging geese. Bring bread and crackers.

Along with a trip to the ocean in winter to watch storms, we have tried to make at least three or four trips a year along the **Arboretum Marshland Nature Trial,** more commonly known as the Foster Island trail. This walk has the bonus

129

of a visit to the **Museum of History and Industry** because it starts at the museum's parking lot, 2161 East Hamlin Street.

The trail begins at a gate put there to discourage bikes (it has only marginal success), since the path is narrow enough to make walkers and bikers an uncomfortable mix. The trail branches almost immediately. One section leads over to the ship canal, the so-called Montlake Cut, which connects Lakes Washington and Union. The trail has a special landscaped platform with seats so you can sit and watch the pleasure boats that parade through the cut every weekend. It continues on beneath the Montlake Bridge, one of the city's many drawbridges. If you're standing beneath it when it is raised to let a tall-masted boat through, you'll see a special view of the bridge.

The other branch of the trail leads out into the marshland along the shore of Lake Washington. It is an elevated, gravel walkway that follows close to the lake, through the reeds and rushes that tower over your head. Frequent turnouts lead to the lakefront with 50-yard-line seats provided to rest

and watch the boats pass by or sit and fish for trout.

The trail ends on Foster Island where more benches and a broad grassy area make a good picnic area. As with Green Lake, the goose and duck population is high and they enjoy their handouts. The round trip is a mile and a half, and the trail is open year-round.

The third in-city hike good year-round is in Lincoln Park at the end of Fauntleroy S.W. The park is a combination of dense timber, open grassy areas for sports, and a great, mile-long stretch of salt-water beach. The park is on a high bluff overlooking the Sound and all the water traffic, and there are only occasional trails carved into the side of the bluff from the beach below. The walk ends at the north border of the park with a switchbacked trail leading back up to the top of the bluff.

This view is from the spur of the Foster Island trail that leads back to the west along the Montlake Cut, which connects Lakes Washington and Union. It is a prime viewpoint during opening day of the yachting season.

One of the best views of the entire city—and Mt. Rainier—is from Kerry Viewpoint on West Highland Drive on Queen Anne Hill with Doris Chase's sculpture, "Changing Form," in the foreground.

The Dream That Failed

There was a time when Port Townsend was considered by nearly everyone in Puget Sound as the most important city in Washington. It was the major terminus for ships, and there was talk of it competing with San Francisco as the most beautiful, gracious city on the West Coast. So important was it that the major governments of the time installed consulates there, along with the beautiful old Victorian homes and government buildings. Lots sold for as much as $500 a front foot in the 1890s. The only thing it needed to become the undisputed shipping capital of the Northwest was a railroad.

The railroad never came, in spite of a huge subsidy guaranteed by the townspeople. That was the beginning of the end for the old Victorian queen city.

For years the city languished. Some of the fine old buildings fell into various states of disrepair. But beginning in the late 1950s and gaining its full momentum in the late 1960s, the town was continually discovered by restoration buffs. Port Townsend is now almost as successful in attracting visitors and investment money as Leavenworth has been across the Cascades.

Many of the old homes and public buildings are open for inspection during the Victorian Home Tour every fall, in either September or October. The Rhododendron Festival the third weekend in May attracts more attention to the 19th century masterpiece.

132

Annual Events

January

Republic—Winter Festival, which includes snowmobile races, sled-dog races, cross-country skiing events
Pullman—Washington State Junior Miss Contest
Bellingham—Robbie Burns Dinner & Dance

February

Tacoma—Washington State Wine Festival
LaConner—Smelt Derby
Chewelah—PNSA Grubstake Giant Slalom at 49 Degrees North
Leavenworth—National Ski Jump Championships
Yakima—Artists of Central Washington Exhibit & Crafts Show
Oak Harbor—Whidbey Island Gem & Mineral Show
Cathlamet—Annual Cherry Pie Festival
Ocean Shores—Fog Festival
Winthrop—World Championship Snowshoe Softball Tournament
49 Degrees North—Ski for Heart & Veterans Race
George—George Washington's Birthday Celebration
Mt. Vernon—George Washington's Birthday Celebration
Toppenish—George Washington's Birthday Celebration
Discovery Bay—Discovery Bay Fire Department Annual Fish Derby
Kennewick—Horse Racing

March

Yakima—Womens' Volleyball Jamboree
Kennewick—Horse racing
Kennewick—Three Rivers Gem & Mineral Show
Yakima—Speelyi-Mi Trade Fair
Snoqualmie Summit—World Pro Ski Races
Spokane—Rockrollers Gem & Mineral Show
Tacoma—Daffodil Coronation
Tenino—Old Time Music Festival
49 Degrees North—PNSA Elite Class Downhill Race
Grayland—Driftwood Show
Fife—Six Foot & Under National Basketball Tournament
Spokane—Auto Boat Speed Show
Prosser—National Chukar Championship Field Trials

Tacoma—PLU Choral Homecoming Concert
Spokane—Diamond Spur Rodeo
Colfax—WSU-Whitman County Horse Show

April

Tacoma-Puyallup-Sumner—Puyallup Valley Daffodil Festival
Moses Lake—Spring Bass Derby (Potholes Reservoir)
Raymond—Parade of Gold Flowers
Bremerton—Regional One-Act Play Competition
Spokane—Lilac Queen Coronation
Dayton—Columbia County Livestock Show
Tacoma—UPS Women's League Flea Market
Ocean Shores—Undiscovery Day
Lynden—International Plowing Match
Yakima—Washington State Old-Time Fiddlers Show
Wenatchee—Washington State Apple Blossom Festival
Oak Harbor—Holland Happening
Spokane—Music & Allied Arts Festival
St. John—St. John Community Fair
Tacoma—Norwegian Arts & Crafts Fair, PLU
Colville—Northeast Washington Fair & Royalty Pageant
Port Orchard—Annual Arts & Historical Festival
Satus—Long House Pow Wow
Spokane—Inland Empire Dog Show
Kennewick—Horse Heaven Hills Appaloosa Horse Sale
Richland—Tri-Cities German Club Mayfest
Long Beach—Loyalty Day Celebration
Port Townsend—Victorian Homes Tour
Ilwaco—Blessing of the Fleet
Spokane—Diamond Spur Rodeo

May

Colfax—All-Arabian Horse Show
Colfax—May Festival
Cathlamet—Annual PTO Smorgasbord
Spokane—Greater Spokane Music & Allied Arts Music Festival
Toppenish—Central Washington Livestock Show
Gig Harbor—Spring Festival of Shops
Pullman—WSU, NIRA Rodeo
Metaline Falls—Dam Hot-Foot Daze

Seattle—Opening of Yacht Season
Kennewick—Sun Downs Quarter Horse Show
Issaquah—Arts Fair
Winthrop—49er Parade and Rodeo
Sequim—Annual Irrigation Festival
Tacoma—Masters of Fine Art Ceramics Exhibit
Spokane—Junior Livestock Show
Grand Coulee—Colorama and Rodeo
Tacoma—UPS Annual Spring Pot and Print Sale
Chehalis—Lewis County Spring Dairy Show
Manson—Manson Apple Blossom Festival
Zillah—Community Day
Bainbridge Island—BISC Dressage Event
Seattle—University District Street Fair
Leavenworth—Mai Fest
Eastsound—Orcas Island Family Festival
Spokane—Spokane Lilac Festival
Cathlamet—Mai Fest
Ocean Park—Clam Diggers Breakfast
Poulsbo—Viking Festival
Lake Samish (Bellingham)—Blossomtime Hobie Cat Regatta
Ballard—Norwegian Independence Day Parade
Shelton—Mason County Forest Festival
Bremerton—Armed Forces Week Observance
Bainbridge Island—Annual PTO Homes Tour
Port Townsend—Rhododendron Festival
Bellingham—Blossomtime "Ski-to-Sea" Festival
Aberdeen—Aberdeen Rain Fair
Enumclaw—Enumclaw Junior Dairy Show
Lynden—Gas Engine Show
Vancouver—Fort Vancouver Ham Air
Waitsburg—Days of Real Sport
Yakima—Yakima Gem & Mineral Show
Tonasket—Rodeo
Kirkland—Homes Tour
Colville—Miss Colville Pageant
Bainbridge Island—Scotch Broom Festival
Seattle Center—Northwest Folklife Festival
Yakima—Washington State Open Horse Show
Moses Lake—Vagabond Air Show

Dayton—Dayton Days
Garfield—May Festival
Kahlotus—Frontier Days

June

Marysville—Puget Sound Junior
 Livestock Show
Spokane—Doll Show & Sale
Everett—Salty Sea Days
Renton—Kiwanis Antique Show
Kahlotus—Kahlotus Days Celebration
Maple Valley—Maple Valley Day &
 Cedar River Boat Race
Bellingham—Bellingham Highland
 Games
Roy—Pioneer Rodeo
Seattle—Fire Festival
Yakima—Poor Man's Art Show
Westport-Grayland—Salmon Derby
White Swan—All Indian Rodeo
Bellingham—Lummi Stommish Water
 Festival
White Swan—Treaty Day Celebration
 & Rodeo
White Swan—TIINOWIT International
 Dancing Competition
Spokane—Square Dance Federation
Quincy—Canal Days
Grays River—Not-Quite-White-Water
 River Run
Colfax—Appaloosa Horse Show
Deming—Logging Show
Blaine—International Peace Arch
 Celebration
Port Townsend—Studio Arts Workshop
Woodland—Planters Day Celebration
Rosalia—Battle Days Celebration
Silverdale—Little Britches Rodeo
Edmonds—Art Festival
Colville—Rodeo
Moses Lake—Tennessee Walker
 Horse Show
Bellevue—Swedish Midsummer Festival
Spokane—Saddlebred Open Horse Show
Marysville—Mary Fest
Spokane—Spokane Dog Training Show
Port Townsend—Chamber Music
 Festival
Lake City—Lake City Queen Contest
Burlington—Berry Dairy Days
Vancouver—Miss Washington Pageant
Marysville—Grand Prix Tricycle Race
Kennewick—All Appaloosa Horse Show
Ocean Shores—SOS (See Ocean Shores)
Toppenish—Toppenish Pow-Wow Days
Auburn—Street Walking Art Fair
Kelso—Hilander Summer Festival

Lakewood Center—Lakewood Summer
 Festival
George—Summer Bass Derby,
 Evergreen Reservoir
Mt. Vernon—Sidewalk Celebration
Darrington—Timber Bowl Rodeo
Ephrata—Freedom Festival
Yakima—Annual Yakima Indian
 Encampment
Colfax—Old-Fashioned Ice Cream Social
Colville—Stevens County Pioneer Picnic
Arlington—Stillaguamish Valley
 Frontier Days
Colfax—Evergreen & Border Quarter
 Horse Show
Sedro Woolley—Loggerodeo

July

(Fourth of July Celebrations—
Everywhere)
Cle Elum—Pioneer Days
Longview—Lower Columbia College
 Arts & Crafts Festival
Oak Harbor—Events & People of the
 Past (July 4)
Yakima—Frank Lovering Memorial
 Baseball Tournament
Spokane—Summer Arts Festival
Mt. Vernon—Skagit River Raft Race
Orcas Island—Historical Society Parade
 & Fireworks
Arlington—Antique Car Show
Colville—Elks July 4 Golf Tournament
Yakima—National AAU, Jr., Olympic
 Pentathlon & Decathlon
Redmond—Marymoor Park Heritage
 Festival
Port Orchard—Fathoms O'Fun
Yakima—Kiwanis Invitational
 Swim Meet
Bellingham—All Breed Dog Show &
 Obedience Trial
Arlington—Run, Bike, Canoe Marathon
Renton—Old-Fashioned Picnic
Winthrop—River Rat Race
Woodinville—County Fair
Port Townsend—Festival of American
 Fiddle Tunes
Westport—Charter Boat Derby
Puyallup—Ezra Meeker Days
Kirkland—Moss Bay Festival
Everson—Junior Rodeo
Langley—Golf Tournament
Olympia—Capital Lakefair
Yakima—All Arabian Horse Show
Auburn—Auburn Air Fair
Spokane—Cheney Rodeo

Lake Whatcom—Hobie Cat Regatta
Colfax—Pioneer Picnic
Port Townsend—Poetry Symposium
Lynnwood—Lynn-O-Rama South City
 Community Festival
Chehalis—Crazy Daze
Mt. Vernon—Skagit Squares Annual
 Conference-Workshop
Spokane—Pacific Sunset Review of Drum
 & Bugle Corps Competition
Battleground—Harvest Days
Chelan—Lake Chelan Rodeo
McCleary—Bear Festival
Renton—Annual Art Show
Belfair—Summer Festival
Ocean Park—Beachcombers Two-Ball
 Golf Tournament
Blaine—Skywater Festival
Everett—Rotary International Air
 Fair (Paine Field)
Bainbridge Island—BISC Invitational
 Horse Show
Mountlake Terrace—Recreation Fair
Port Angeles—Arts in Action
Silverdale—Whaling Days
Seattle—Pacific Northwest Festival
 (Wagner's "Ring" Cycle)
Ballard—Sidewalk Sale
Bellevue—Pacific Northwest Arts and
 Crafts Festival
Kalama—Community Fair
Richland—Tri-Cities Water Follies
Bremerton—Air Fair
Cathlamet—Logging Show
Pateros—Apple Pie Jamboree
Renton—Arts & Crafts Festival
Seattle International District—Bon
 Odori
Port Townsend—Science Fiction
 Workshop
Soap Lake—Suds & Sun
Kent-Seattle—National Bicycle
 Championships Road Trials
Ferndale—Old Settlers Annual Picnic
Richland—Allied Arts Annual Sidewalk
 Show
Oak Harbor—North Whidbey Stampede
Ilwaco—Shriners Afifi Fish Derby
Anacortes—An-O-Chords Annual Bight
 of Harmony & Bar-B-Que
Buckley—Old Timer Days
Steilacoom—Historical Museum Salmon
 Bake
Richland—Gold Cup Hydroplane Races
Port Townsend—Summer Dance Lab
Seattle—Seafair Week
Tri-Cities—Waterfollies Hydro Races
Kennewick—Tumbleweed Rodeo &
 County Fair

August

Port Townsend—Theater Experience
Des Moines—Waterland Festival
LaConner—Skagit County Pioneer
Picnic
Sumner—Sumner Festival
Lake City—Pioneer Days Parade
Cheney—Cheney Festival
Lake City—Salmon Barbecue
Whidbey Island—Air Show &
Open House
Bothell—Highland Games
Clarkston—Snake River Days
Colville—P.Q.H.A. Junior Rodeo
Anacortes—Arts & Crafts Festival
Vancouver—International Festival
Fort Flagler—Marrowstone Music
Festival
Custer—YWCA Annual Golf
Tournament
Ilwaco—Flea Market
Omak—Omak Stampede & Suicide Race
Redmond—Bicycle Derby
Orcas Island—Arts & Crafts Fair & Sale
Morton—Loggers Jubilee
Yakima—Eastern Washington Junior
Horse Show
Long Beach—Saddle Club Rodeo
Spokane—Inland Empire Arabian Horse
Show
Bellevue—Begonia Show
Ilwaco—Ilwaco Charter Association
Salmon Derby
Spokane—Appaloosa Horse Show
Bainbridge Island—BISC Canal Zone
Horse Show
Port Townsend—Salmon Derby
Kitsap County Fair & Rodeo—Poulsbo
Fairgrounds
Graham—Hamfair
Leavenworth—Chelan County Old
Timers Picnic
Kennewick—Sun Downs RCA Rodeo
Bellingham—Mt. Baker Quarter
Horse Show
Lynden—Threshing Bee

Neah Bay—Makah Days
Lacey—Music-Arts-Dance Festival
Ellensburg—National Western Art Show
and Auction
Richland—Washington Old-Time
Fiddlers Campout
Olympia—Pet Parade
Seattle—Dahlia and Rose Show
Tacoma—Washington State Dahlia
Society Show
Seattle—Bumbershoot Arts Festival
Richland—Pacific NW PGA
Championship

September

Port Angeles—Salmon Derby Days
Kennewick—Fun-in-the-Sun Rod Run
Ocean Park—Peninsula Art Festival
Ellensburg—Rodeo
Winthrop Rodeo
Langley—Arts & Crafts Festival
Pullman—Labor Day Picnic
Prosser—States Day Celebration
Renton—Poor Man Show
Seattle—Ceramic Art Association Show
Hoquiam—Logger's Playday
Long Beach—Cranberry Festival &
Street Fair
Moses Lake—AKC Dog Show
Sunnyside—Sunshine Days
Richland—Beaux Arts Starving Artists
Sale & Auction
Burien—Medieval Festival
Wenatchee—Apple Valley Street Fair
Odessa—Odessa Deutsches Fest
Ballard—Seafood Fest
Harrah—Sugar Beet Festival
Moses Lake—Fall Bass Derby
Winthrop—Antique Auto Show
Port Townsend—Victorian Homes Tour
Waitsburg—Pioneer Fall Festival
White Swan—National Indian Day
Celebration
Burien—Miss Burien Scholarship
Pageant

Ocean Shores—Art Festival
Bainbridge Island—Bainbridge Broncs
4-H Canal Zone Horse Show
Ocean Shores—Beaux Arts Ball
Spokane—Shrine Football Game
Ocean Park—Beachcombers Two-Ball
Golf Tournament
Leavenworth—Autumn Leaf Festival
Bainbridge Island—BISC State
Horse Show
Bremerton—Peninsula Dog
Fanciers Show
Monroe—Draft Horse Extravaganza
Yakima—Sun Fair
Richland—Oktoberfest
Chelan—Lake Chelan Sailing Regatta
Colfax—Palouse Empire Fair
Wellpinit—Spokane Indian Days
Ellensburg—Rodeo
Walla Walla—Southeastern
Washington Fair
Puyallup—Western Washington Fair

October

Spokane Valley—Hearts of Gold
Festival & Parade
Issaquah—Salmon Days
Spokane—Antique & Collectors Sale
Colville—P.Q.H.A. Open Horse Show
Tacoma—Scandinavian Days
Mt. Vernon—Colonial Banquet
Bothell—Bracket's Haunted Barn
Cheney—EWSC Homecoming
Colville—Halloween Parade
Poulsbo—Lutefisk Dinner

December

Seattle—Museum of History & Industry,
Christmas Around the World
Seattle—Kingbowl State High School
Football Championships
Leavenworth—Christmas Lighting
Festival
Snoqualmie—Snoqualmie Valley
Christmas Village
Olympia—Christmas Island

136

Index